And God Gave Women Talents!

And God Gave Women Talents!

Marlys Taege

Concordia®
Publishing House
St. Louis

Concordia Publishing House, St. Louis, Missouri

MANUFACTURED IN THE UNITED STATES OF AMERICA

Library of Congress Cataloging in Publication Data

Taege, Marlys, 1928-
And God gave women talents!

Bibliography: p.
1. Women—Religious life. 2. Women in church work. 3. Women in Christianity. I. Title.
BV4527.T33 261.8'34'12 78-968
ISBN 0-570-03775-1

Acknowledgments

Scripture quotations marked TEV are used by permission of American Bible Society, from the *Good News Bible,* copyright © TEV, 1966, 1971, 1976.

Scripture quotations marked RSV are from the Revised Standard Version of the Bible, copyrighted 1946, 1952, © 1971, 1973.

Scripture quotations marked MLB are from *The Modern Language Bible, The New Berkeley Version in Modern English.* Copyright © 1959 © 1969 by Zondervan Publishing House. Used by permission.

The poem "Lord, send me a surprise" is reprinted from *Surprise Me, Jesus* by Herbert F. Brokering © 1973, by permission of Augsburg Publishing House.

The quotations chapter 7 from the book *Women: From the Greeks to the French Revolution* by Susan Groag Bell are used by permission of Wadsworth Publishing Co., Inc., Belmont, CA.

The quotations chapter 8 from *Women on a Mission* by Ruth Fritz Meyer, © LWML, 1967, are used by permission.

The quotations chapter 7 from the book *Great Women of the Christian Faith,* Edith Deen, Harper & Row, New York, 1976. Used by permission of the author.

Dedicated to
my daughters, Linda and Lauren,
and my son, James,
who have understood and shared
the struggles, the clutter,
and the excitement
of each editorial deadline . . .
and to my husband, Jack,
whose love helped me discover
who I am.

Contents

Introduction

"I ALWAYS KNEW those clippings I've been collecting would come in handy some day!" This half-joking remark was my initial response to the request to write a book about women's role in the church. With more than 20 years background as a writer and editor for a Lutheran women's organization, I thought I had a fair amount of knowledge about the subject. As I began doing research, however, I was amazed at what I learned. For instance:

—I knew that life over the centuries had been a struggle for women because men relegated them to prescribed roles. I didn't realize how difficult this fact had made life for women in some cultures.

—I knew there were many examples of strong women in the Bible. I didn't realize how many. I discovered several I never knew existed.

—As a speaker for years on the subject "Who Am I?" I knew many women have trouble answering this question for themselves today. I didn't realize how *long* women have been asking themselves this very thing. I didn't realize how long the desire for self-identity had been simmering, how long women have been seeking greater opportunity to use their God-given talents in His service.

I did know the Bible offers great freedom through Christ, but unfortunately many women—and men—are not aware of what it actually says. It is my hope that this book will bring God's Word to bear on the subject in a way which will help women understand who they are and enable the church to more fully use their talents so God's will may be done on earth.

So much has already been written on the subject that one may be tempted to ask, "What more could be said?" Most of what has been published, however, has been written by learned women theologians and by rabid women's rightists. This book, I hope, will speak to the woman in the pew, to the pastor who counsels her, and the man who encourages her. Many doors are open to the woman in the parish. And, many people—three billion of them—still do not know Christ. How can the Christian woman find her role, her mission, and fulfill it? Where does she fit in history, in God's plan, and in the church? Now is the time to find those answers. Let's seek them together.

1

Who Am I?

CONFUSED! Perhaps that word best describes today's Christian woman as she struggles with the question, "Who am I?"

Ask the members of a church women's group to think of five answers to that question, and puzzled frowns cross the majority of the faces. Ask them also to list three of their talents, and the immediate response is "What if I don't have any?"

(How about you? What would you say if you were to ask yourself, "Who am I? What are my talents?")

The confusion is understandable. New opportunities are opening daily for women as members of our sex succeed in new jobs . . . astronaut, speedway driver, TV news anchor, airline pilot, bank president, business executive, tennis pro. The bold shout, "Bravo!" and climb onward.

But others, repulsed by the bra-burners and the extremities of the equal rights movement, find themselves on the teeter-totter between tradition and adventure. "Do I really want all that I can have today? What price must I pay for it—and what will be the cost to future generations?" these woman ask. Homemaking and motherhood are important, too, they emphasize.

Still others, trapped in their roles by lack of education, by past failures and "put-downs," by timidity and a seeming lack of talents, recoil in fear from today's challenges. Other women's successes pose a threat to their self-image. Opportunities become obstacles as they conclude, "I can't cope. I don't measure up."

But the problem for women goes beyond the matter of new roles and the question of new ideals. Self-realization is difficult for anyone, male or female, in today's society. We live in an age of insecurity, an age when it's so easy to say:

—I'm just a number.

Ask any widow and she'll tell you, "After my husband died, I went to the Social Security office and told them my name, but they were more interested in his Social Security number, my Social Security number, and whether my children had Social Security numbers. At the Veterans Administration office, the most important thing was his veteran's number. At the bank, it was his checking account number and his savings account number."

Everyone, not just a widow, encounters the numbers game daily. The Post Office has its zip codes. Area codes rather than city names are basic to telephoning. Credit card companies want the member's card number written on every payment check. The phone company requests the user's phone number on all correspondence. Cashing a check at the store requires a driver's license number or a store registration number.

"A number—that's all I am," is the logical conclusion. "My name doesn't matter. I'm not important!"

—I'm outdated!

Toeffler's "future shock" isn't *future* anymore. It's here NOW. Change confronts us daily. Nothing seems permanent.

We live in a throw-away society. Most containers are disposable; glass milk bottles have become collector's items. Appliance manufacturers urge buyers to take out insurance in case repairs are needed the first year. Automobile agencies advertise, "Don't buy a car—rent one."

Builders talk of "planned obsolescence"—a big word which simply means that in the future houses will be built to be torn down in 25 years. Bulldozers will level entire subdivisions to make way for new construction. Not only will this provide more jobs but it will enable homeowners to utilize modern materials.

Moreover, the average American moves once in every seven years. Children thus have little sense of roots. One member of a historical society says she joined to make sure future generations will have a heritage of more than hamburger joints and jukeboxes.

Lifestyles are changing too. Divorce is on the increase. Abortions outnumber adoptions in major cities. Communal living experiments are on the rise, and laws are being changed to legalize the cohabitation of an unmarried man and woman.

According to a recent newscast, only 7 percent of today's households are traditional, with a father who works outside the home and a mother who stays home to care for the children. Most mothers hold paying jobs, and many households consist only of single, widowed, or divorced persons.

"Everything's changing too fast" is the conclusion.

"What can I hang on to? Maybe I just don't fit in this age" is the fear.

—*I'm nothing.* This is the person who says, "I don't have any talents. I'm all thumbs when it comes to doing things. I feel like a mindless blob when I read about a computer that can remember millions of items, and I sometimes forget to put my shopping list in my purse. I feel worthless when I see on television that men are walking on the moon, that broadcasts from other continents are coming into my home via satellite, that scientific equipment has been landed on Mars. The calculations required to accomplish this boggle my mind! Why, I have trouble following a recipe!"

"What value have I, a poor worthless being? Why am I here?" is the cry.

Christians are particularly prone to the "I'm nothing" syndrome. We have grown up learning that we are "by nature sinful and unclean," so we think we can't do anything right. Moreover, we know that pride is a sin, so we hesitate to think, much less say, that we have talents and abilities. (Besides, if we think we don't have any talents, then we can't be expected to use them in serving others. And that saves us lots of hassles!)

We forget that it is not pride to admit God has given us talents. Our gifts are not due to any merit or worthiness in us but to the creativity and grace of our Lord. When we claim we have no talents, we are really saying, "Lord, when you made me, you did a bum job." But our Lord never does a poor job!

Discovering who I am, though, derives its value not simply from acknowledging God's creative ability. Knowing who I am and why I'm here is important for each of us as individuals and for those whose lives we touch, because the results of insecurity are numerous and demoralizing. They lead to strained relationships and false ways of achieving self-importance. These include:

—*Gossip.* People gossip to move themselves one step up the ladder by pushing someone else down. When a woman cattily remarks, "Wow! Did you see Suzy's new hairdo?" what she's really saying is, "My hair looks better than hers!"

And when she says, "That dress makes Joan look like a tub!" what she means is, "My dress is more stylish and more becoming!" or "My figure is much slimmer!" Translation: "I have better taste than she does. I'm nicer looking than she is."

—*Criticism and counter-criticism* ("an eye for an eye"). Insecurity leads to the desire to criticize and dominate others and to insistence that things be done my way. (When people do as I say, that proves I know best!) Couple that outlook with inability to accept advice or assistance, no matter how well-intentioned it may be, and the situation becomes explosive. Example: "Please, Mother, I'd rather do it myself!"

Even a concerned question or comment may trigger a sarcastic response and result in a verbal sparring match. "You look tired," says one spouse. The other retorts, "You don't look so great yourself!" And they're off!

Or the husband asks, "Why isn't dinner ready?" "Well," answers his wife, "If some people wouldn't dirty so many clothes and wear so many holes in their socks, and if some people's children weren't so naughty, they might get their meals on time!"

Feeling diminished by the question, the wife thus responds with a put-down. Because she has a poor self-image, she immediately assumes the worst connotation and sees the question as a criticism of her housekeeping ability. She might respond differently had she asked herself, "What's behind his question? Is it simply that he's hungry, or did his boss give him a rough time?"

—*Prejudice.* An age-old way of bolstering egos is through pre-judging another person because of factors over which she has no control. When we suggest that one nationality is miserly, that one color is dirty, or one race is stupid, we are really patting ourselves on the back and saying, "My race is more intelligent than hers. My nationality is more lovable." As we move someone down in the eyes of others, we move ourselves up in our own estimation—but the base is a weak one, for there is no race, no color, no nationality to which humiliating labels have not been attached by someone.

—*Jealousy.* Even the church is not without it! The organist plays too fast. The soloist thinks she's a prima donna. The pastor is friendlier to Mrs. Jones than he is to me. Mrs. Brown always wants to run everything. The list could go on and on.

We're jealous because we think others have more talents. Yet the Bible tells us we are all created by God. All have been given talents. Add up all the skills and abilities of the members of the parish, and we have a glimpse of what our beautiful Savior is like. His voice is melodic and persuasive; the touch of His hand is warm and friendly; He is the perfect organizer. Yes, His attributes are visible in His creation if we can forget about ourselves long enough to look at His world. When we fail to appreciate others, we miss a vision of our Lord.

—*Loneliness.* Depression and anxiety abound today. We worry about the future, the present, and the things we have done in the past. In bitterness and frustration we isolate ourselves. Rather than seeking people who can help, we believe no one wants to listen. It's easier to sit and suffer than risk and compete. We don't like the heat, so we get out of the fire, forgetting that in the fire is also warmth and companionship and friendship. To be alone is our choice . . . all alone . . . frozen to immobility.

And it's all so unnecessary—at least for a Christian.

Christians have no need to build themselves up by demeaning others. No need to gossip, prejudge, or criticize to gain self-importance. No need to be jealous or lonely. They have the promises of our Lord: I will be with you always to the end of the earth. You are mine. I made you. You have talents.

Yet how difficult some churchmen have made it for women to overcome these tendencies! Through misapplied doctrinal interpretations and Scriptural emphases, these spiritual leaders have often failed to convey the fact that women, too, can "do all things through Christ, which strengtheneth me."

For instance, Christ told women to go and tell, but most churches throughout history have placed greater emphasis on the Biblical directive to keep silent.

1 Corinthians 12 indicates that women too receive gifts important to the body of Christ, but church customs for centuries have caused women to bury many of their talents.

Ephesians points out that all persons are His workmanship, created for good works which our Lord had in mind for us even before we were born. Yet the church has often stressed woman's uncleanness, viewed her as weak and unstable, and relegated her to second-class citizenship in the Christian community.

The Bible contains numerous examples of outstanding women, but rarely are such passages the basis of sermons, and rarely are these women (with the possible exception of Mary) portrayed in church art or stained glass windows.

God Himself placed a woman over His people as a ruler, but until 1977 one Lutheran college maintained the practice of having the college president (a man) function as head of the college ladies' aid.

The dilemma facing Christian women was dramatized at one workshop by a skit entitled "Anatomy Is Destiny" and a filmstrip on the masculinity of our worship language. Together they illustrated the sharp contrast between what life in the church is like today and what some fear it will become if women's rightists have their way. Together they demonstrated the extremes that can occur when the pendulum swings too far—and it is fear of the one extreme that causes some people to accept the other extreme.

Set in the 21st century, the skit portrays a time when woman is the dominant sex, and man is known as no-woman. Since "function determines role," according to Margaret Mead, the physically stronger no-woman stays home and handles the mundane but more tiring routines of daily living. A newspaper no-woman, the author of "The Masculine Mistaque," is interviewing Peter, the househusband of the renowned astrophysicist, Henrietta Jean Cosby.

Peter reveals how he gave up a very promising career in architecture after taking a good look at his cousin Alfred, who "is 30 now and hasn't snared himself a woman yet." Alfred never learned that "it's not smart to be too smart," and scared off all his prospects for marriage.

"I'm glad I found true fulfillment," says Peter, as the children come home from school and he makes them peanut butter sandwiches.

The youngsters begin building toy rockets, and the boy says to his sister, "When I grow up, I'm going to be a space-woman." Peter corrects him: "No, honey, when you grow up, you're going to be a househusband, just like Daddy."

The filmstrip, on the other hand, portrays two women in church, one a member, the other a first-time guest. As the congregation begins singing "Faith of Our Fathers," the guest asks, "Don't you sing about mothers too?" "Oh," says the hostess, "*fathers* includes *mothers*."

During the next hymn, "Sons of God," the guest again nudges her friend and asks, "What about the daughters?" "We understand that *sons* includes *daughters*," says the member.

As the word "men" is sung frequently during the final hymn, the guest knowingly whispers, "And, of course, *men* includes *women*!" Her hostess beams in approval.

Then the filmstrip pauses briefly, and the concluding scene shows a very red-faced guest a few minutes after the end of the service. In the background are two doors. She is coming out of one, saying, "Well, I see your church has one place where *men* does not include *women*!"

Yes, the answer is "CONFUSED" when a woman today asks: "Who am I?" Never before have women had so many challenges and opportunities, so many possible goals and ideals, so many conflicting voices offering advice. Never before has the need been so great for women to answer that question for themselves so that they can be all the Lord intended them to be and accomplish all He had in mind for them to do for His people and His cause.

How can the church help them find the answers? Must the church accommodate itself to all the demands of equal rights proponents? Or, should it advocate withdrawal from that movement of society?

To find the answers requires a look at history, both in the church and the nation. It requires an understanding of both liberation and wholeness, of affirmation and authority, of the implications of mission and ministry—and above all, a knowledge of what the Bible says about women and to women.

2

I Am God's Creation

You created every part of me; You put me together in my mother's womb.

Ps. 139:13 TEV

There are different abilities to perform service, but the same God gives ability to everyone for their particular service. The Spirit's presence is shown in some way in each person for the good of all.

1 Cor. 12:6, 7 TEV

Live life, then, with a due sense of responsibility, not as those who do not know the meaning and purpose of life, but as those who do. Make the best use of your time, despite all the difficulties of these days. Don't be vague, but firmly grasp what you know to be the will of God.

Eph. 5:15 Phillips

WHAT IS THE WILL of God for me? How do I know it? How do I recognize it? What direction does the Bible give me? How can I love myself—and others—if I don't know myself? What is woman? Who am I?

Those questions have plagued women, and men, since the beginning of time, and yet the answers have been there in the pages of Holy Scripture.

The first and most obvious answer for all human beings is that we, men and women, are God's creation.

> Then God said, "And now We will make human beings; they will be like Us and resemble Us. They will have power over the fish, the birds and all animals, domestic and wild, large and small." So God created human beings, making them to be like Himself. He created them male and female, blessed them and said, "Have many children, so that your descendants will live all over the earth and bring it under their control."
>
> Gen. 1:26-28 TEV

Yes, we are made by God, and His directive to women as well as men is to have dominion over the earth. Women, too, are to participate in the process of bringing it under control. It is an active, not a passive role that is here prescribed for women. We are to be doers of the Word, not hearers only.

Even more important we (male and female) are made by God in His image. A woman in the image of our masculine Lord? Perhaps we do not consider this fact because so much Biblical language is masculine. However, the image of God is spiritual, not physical. We should not forget that human words cannot adequately describe this all-knowing and all-present Lord of ours.

Nor should we forget that the Bible also uses feminine descriptives and metaphors to help us understand God more fully. In Proverbs the word "wisdom" is personified in the feminine. (The Hebrew word for wisdom is *hokmah,* feminine in gender.) Thus we have passages like:

> Blessed is the man who has found wisdom, . . . She

> is more valuable than jewels. . . . Length of days is in her right hand, riches and honor in her left. . . . She is a tree of life to those laying hold of her, making happy each one holding her fast. The Lord by wisdom founded the earth; by understanding He established the heavens.
>
> Prov. 3:13, 15, 16, 18-19 MLB

> Get wisdom. . . . Do not forsake her and she will protect you; love her, and she will guard you. . . . Exalt her and she will lift you up.
>
> Prov. 4:5, 6, 8 MLB

In Deut. 32:18 (RSV), God takes on the nature of a mother: "You forgot the God who gave you birth."

In Isaiah 42:14 (TEV), God says, "I cry out like a woman in labor," and in 66:13, "I will comfort you in Jerusalem, as a mother comforts her child."

Christ also uses feminine images to refer to Himself. Speaking to the people of Jerusalem, He says with motherly warmth and concern, "How many times I wanted to put my arms around all your people, just as a hen gathers her chicks under her wings, but you would not let Me!" (Matt. 23:37 TEV). In His parable of the lost coin our Lord not only identifies Himself with the woman in the lost coin story, but He presents her as an example for us to follow in seeking the lost: "Suppose a woman who has 10 silver coins loses one of them—what does she do? She lights a lamp, sweeps her house, and looks carefully everywhere until she finds it" (Luke 15:8 TEV).

According to the Hebrew Christian author Richard Wurmbrand, Christ's name in Hebrew (Jeshua) is also feminine. "It is as though we were to call a boy Helen or Katherine. A man with a female name. It was this mystery which was expressed in the outward appearance of an Orthodox priest: He had to have a beard, but wear a woman's robe."[1]

The point of this discussion is not to create an argument about the maleness or femaleness of the Lord, nor to give credence to the claim of some women that God is "She," but to help us understand as Wurmbrand says, "God has all the perfections; he cannot be limited to the male ones."[2]

As woman understands the nature of the Lord, her life, her faith—and her creation—take on new meaning. The Lord who dwells in the temple of her body becomes one with her in a very special and personal way.

Created by God, woman is no accident. She is no "misbegotten male," as Aristotle suggested. Rather she is fashioned by the Lord, handcrafted by Him. "From the rib He had taken from the man, God formed a woman" (Gen. 2:22 MLB).

This fact led Margaret of Navarre (she is known as the "godmother of the Reformation" because her palace was a haven for the French reformers) to believe that woman is the ultimate of God's creation. Woman, she said, is "the masterpiece of God since she was formed after man and was God's last work." She added that women have intuitive powers lacking to men; therefore they are more intelligent. Also, she said, women should be able to command more effectively because they are more willing to listen and therefore more reasonable.[3]

Scripture, however, does not support her conclusions. Rather, the Genesis creation account portrays man and woman as comparable and complementary.

The Lord God said: It is not good for the man to be alone; I will make him a suitable helper, completing him" (Gen. 2:18 MLB). Without woman, man was incomplete. Woman is necessary, not just for procreation, but for oneness and wholeness. She is bone of his bone, flesh of his flesh—they are one.

As God looked at all that He created prior to human beings, He saw that it was *good*, but as He looked at man *and* woman, He saw that this creation was *excellent*. I—woman—am an excellent creation of God! As Luther says in his explanation to the first article of the Apostles' Creed, my creation by the Lord means that "He has given me my body and soul, eyes, ears, and all my members, my reason and all my senses, and still preserves them." He even knows the number of hairs on my head—now that's familiarity! That's personal interest! That's firsthand knowledge! That's an almighty God who cares!

And He assures me that I am precious to Him. Not even a sparrow is forgotten in God's presence, Luke tells us (12:6), and I am "worth more than *flocks* of sparrows." That's value multiplied!

But my value comes not because of anything I have done or could do but rather because "we are His workmanship, created in Christ Jesus for good works, which God prepared beforehand, that we should walk in them" (Eph. 2:10 RSV). That word *workmanship* in the original Greek can also be translated *poetry*. Each of us is a poem, not ordinary prose, not the ordinary language that we speak, but poetry, written by God Himself and placed here on earth so that all who see us can see something of the great grace and love of God, something of His beauty and glory. What a reason for being!

But there's more! Even before we were born, God

had good works in mind for us, this verse tells us. No life is without purpose. Everyone, each woman included, has a reason for existing.

It's so easy, though, to get hung up on what that reason is. All our lives we Christians are told what sinners we are—and that's true, for we all sin daily—but the problem is that we can become immobilized by the thought of sin. We think we are no good, of no worth. We come to believe we can't do anything right. Everyone else seems better, richer, happier, more blest. We are "chief of sinners."

What we forget is that in the body of Christ, all are important (and all believers *are* a part of that body).

> Christ is like a single body, which has many parts; it is still one body, even though it is made up of different parts. In the same way, all of us, whether Jews or Gentiles, whether slaves or free, have been baptized into the one body by the same Spirit, and we have all been given the one Spirit to drink. For the body itself is not made up of only one part, but of many parts. . . . We cannot do without the parts of the body that seem to be weaker. . . . If one part of the body suffers, all the other parts suffer with it.
>
> 1 Cor. 12:12-14, 22, 26 TEV

It matters not whether you are a hand, a foot, a knee or a fleck of skin. Each has a purpose, a role to perform. That point was brought home to me one day when I scuffed my bare foot against the edge of a piece of paper, just barely knicking a fleck of skin on the bottom of one toe. The next day the toe was sore and I felt it with every step I took. My entire body was affected as I walked—simply because that tiny layer of skin was unable to perform its protective role. The role planned for each man—and each woman—even before we were born, is important to the total body of Christ.

Being created by a loving God, we can be sure that He has given, or will give, us the talents and skills necessary for every job He has in mind for us. If you think you have no talents, maybe for you it's like the story which Corrie ten Boom tells. When you were a child and going on a train trip, she asks, when did your father give you your ticket—three weeks ahead of time, or just as you were boarding the train? So it is with the Lord, she concludes. When He calls you to perform a task, even to be a martyr, He will give you the ability and courage you need at exactly the right time.

Sometimes we think that it's wrong to admit we have talents. That's exhibiting pride, we say, and pride is a sin. Let's remember that it is not pride to acknowledge that the Lord has given us abilities. They are ours not because we deserve them but because they are necessary for the work we are to do in His kingdom.

Women who were present at the founding of the Lutheran Women's Missionary League in Chicago in 1942 had to be reminded of that fact too. As woman after woman was nominated for national office in the new organization, each declined, feeling that she wasn't qualified. Finally a counselor took the floor and said: "When the Lord taps you on the shoulder and says, 'I need you for this job,' you must not turn Him down. If He did not think you could do it, He would not have asked you."

Our Lord gives us this promise:

> To each is granted the evidence of the Spirit for the common welfare. To one person is given by the Spirit a message of wisdom and to another the utterance of

knowledge according to the same Spirit; to a third faith is granted by the same Spirit; to yet another the gifts of healing by the one Spirit; to another miraculous powers; to this one prophecy, to that one discrimination between spirits, to a third variety of tongues, and to yet another the ability to interpret tongues. All these abilities one and the same Spirit energizes, distributing to each individual exactly as He pleases.

1 Cor. 12:7-11 MLB

There's nothing partisan or chauvinist about that passage, nothing to indicate that men will get the better abilities and women the lesser; in fact, nothing to suggest that one ability is better and another lesser.

We all receive talents, men *and* women.

We all are important, men *and* women.

We all are His creation, place here for a purpose.

That makes you really special. That makes me really special. Knowing that, I can love myself—and others as I love myself. Knowing that, I can firmly grasp what God, not man, reveals as His will for me, for He made me and He gives me His power.

It's like another Corrie ten Boom story. She tells of a woodpecker pecking a tree, not making much progress. Suddenly a bolt of lightening hit the tree, splitting it in two. "Wow," exclaimed the woodpecker, "I didn't know I had that power within me."

Women have that power—and today they know it! The question is: What are they doing with it? What are you doing with yours?

3

I Am a Christian

For ye are all the children of God by faith in Christ Jesus. For as many of you as have been baptized into Christ have put on Christ. There is neither Jew nor Greek, there is neither bond nor free, there is neither male nor female: for ye are all one in Christ Jesus.

Gal. 3:26-28 KJ

You are the chosen race, the King's priests, the holy nation, God's own people, chosen to proclaim the wonderful acts of God, who called you out of darkness into His own marvelous light.

1 Peter 2:9 TEV

It is for freedom that Christ has set us free.

Gal. 5:1 NIV

You are free from the law, but that doesn't mean you are free to do wrong. Live as those who are free to do only God's will at all times.

1 Peter 2:16 Living Bible

WHEN GOD CREATED Adam and Eve, He did not make robots. He gave them free will, and they made the wrong choice. They ate the forbidden fruit. (I'm always thankful that Eve at least argued with the snake a bit, reminding him of God's directive. Regarding Adam, the Bible simply says that Eve "gave some to her husband, and he also ate it.") Yes, they both sinned—Eve first and then Adam.

When God questioned them, the man blamed the woman and the woman blamed the snake. How often we do the same. We lie, cheat, overindulge, fail to use our time wisely, and then blame our parents, teachers, pastors, and anyone who had an influence on our lives. We deserve death.

Praise God, because He understands us (He created us!) and He loves us still. His love becomes evident immediately in the garden as He realizes that Adam and Eve "must not be allowed to eat fruit from the tree of life, and live forever" (Gen. 3:22 TEV). Because they had sinned, because they had fallen, God realized they could not be trusted to refrain from eating the fruit of the tree of life. If they ate that fruit, they would live forever on earth. To live forever in this sinful world, without the hope of heaven, would be disaster. So God sent them "out of the Garden of Eden. . . . Then at the east side of the garden he put living creatures and a flaming sword which turned in all directions. This was to keep anyone from coming near the tree of life" (Gen. 3:23, 24 TEV).

And then He promised a Savior, a pathway to heaven, a promise which He kept with the birth of Jesus. So often we who have been Christians all our life tend to take Christ for granted. We tend to forget or ignore the agony of Calvary, the greatness of the gift.

Take a moment to think about it right now. What would your life be like without Christ—or what could your life be like with Christ?

Christ is God's *only* Son. Through Christ, this great God took on human nature, endured suffering and shame for you and me. As I look at my son, I know I couldn't do this. I don't have that kind of love. I couldn't give up my child to die for all the sinners in this world, the thieves, murderers, and cheats, the unkind and unloving. Yet God did just that—He sent His only Son to a creation that had rejected Him, sent Him so that all who believe could have eternal life.

All includes *you* and *me,* and by His action at Calvary, God declared our worth. God said, "You are important. I love you. I want you as My own forever. My Son will pay for all your sins. All you have to do is believe."

What value that places on me! Not only am I God's creation, but I am also His redeemed child. The Son of God gave His life for me. That's importance!

What does that mean for this lifetime on earth? What does it mean to answer the question "Who am I?" by saying, "I am a Christian"?

It means that my sins are forgiven. When I sin and repent, my forgiveness is complete. It's like the robe which the pastor wears in many churches—the white covers the black. Christ envelopes us so that when our Lord looks at us, He sees Christ and not our sins.

And that's true whether we are men or women, for in Christ there is neither male nor female. There's no discrimination here—only freedom, regardless of sex, nationality, or station in life.

We are free because Christ set us free, free to love God and people, free to forgive because we know we are forgiven, free to accept ourselves because God has accepted us, free to be what God created us to be, free to serve, free to share, free to come to God.

In gratitude we become His servants, His slaves—not because we have to but because we want to. In gratitude we serve others, not to prove to them that Christianity makes a difference, not to validate the Gospel, but because we are thankful for what the Lord has done for us, and we want to show our appreciation to God. In gratitude we serve others, not to work our way to heaven, for it is ours through faith, but because good works are the fruit of faith. "Faith without works is dead."

Moved to such love, the Christian community becomes like mashed potatoes. If you pick some potatoes and put them in a pail, there is a certain togetherness. If you peel those potatoes, cut them up and put them in a pot, there is more togetherness. But when you cook these potatoes and mash them up, that's real togetherness. Christ offers a "mashed potatoes" oneness to each of us; we in turn are to have a "mashed potatoes" concern for all our fellow human beings.

Too often we tend to view the Christian life like a baseball player who wants to return to the dugout as soon as he makes it to first base. We think that when we get to the first base of Christianity, when we know Christ as Savior, that's all there is. As we move to second base, we meet that community of mashed potato Christians, among whom there is no east, west, north, south—no male or female. Here we have fellowship and grow in Christ.

Then it's on to third base where, moved by the agape love of our Lord, we share His love in word and deed with everyone whose life comes in contact with ours. We know that whatever we do to others, we do to the Lord. But no Christian should stay on third base forever.

What we need to remember is that home plate is heaven, and heaven requires reservations (faith in Christ). If we really care about others, we'll share this message with them so that they too can enjoy heaven. So often, though, when it comes to sharing, the idea of evangelism frightens us. "I can't talk about my faith. I don't know what to say" is our excuse. Perhaps we equate evangelism only with door-to-door pests who interrupt us when we want to rest or have something boiling on the stove.

I did too until a Jehovah's Witness came to my door one day. After she talked a bit, I told her of the joy which I have in Christ, the peace which my faith brings. She asked what church I belong to and whether we ever do calling such as her church does. "Yes," I said, "we have an evangelism committee that coordinates periodic canvasses and calls on prospects." Longingly and a bit accusingly, she said, "No one ever called on me." Then she turned abruptly and walked to the car where the others were waiting for her. *They* did come, she seemed to be saying, and now it's too late for me to change.

Of course, because the Lord does give each of us different talents, not all find it easy to carry the message door to door—but all of us can do something. With its 50 workshops on evangelism, the International Congress on World Evangelization, held in Lausanne, Switzerland, in 1974 surely proved that there are many ways of sharing God's Good News.

Workshops varied from writing to research, from

TV programming to newspaper advertising, from crusades to visiting with your neighbors, from youth work to nursing homes to Bible study to women's organizations to the handicapped and on and on. There is a way for each of us, women and men, to share the Good News with others.

Sometimes we offer the excuse that a loving God would not let any of His people go to hell anyway—so why all the effort? We forget that it is not God, but mankind, that created the chasm between heaven and earth. It is God who built the bridge—Christ. Without that bridge, there is not one of us who can make it across the crevice to heaven. All the good works in the world won't do it, despite God's love for us. Faith seems such an easy solution, but sometimes the simplest answer is the most difficult for the human mind to comprehend. The fact is: Any sin is sin, and heaven demands perfection. We can enter only when clothed in Christ's righteousness.

But we can enter, and thanks to Christ, we can come to God directly in prayer, repentance, and love. We don't need a human intercessor, for Christ is our mediary. We don't need to offer sacrifices as people did in Old Testament times, for Christ was our sacrifice, once and for all time. What this means is that all of us—men and women—are priests!

Surely a study of the implications of the priesthood of all believers is needed today as our churches flounder to define the role of woman, the role of man, and the role of pastor.

Pointing to Martin Luther as the champion of the priesthood of all believers, religious historian Philip Schaff defines such priesthood as

> the right and duty of every believer to read the Word of God in his vernacular tongue, to go directly to the throne of grace, and to take an active part in all the affairs of the church according to his peculiar gift and calling. . . . The principle of the general priesthood of the Christian people is the true source of religious and civil freedom.[4]

In a commemorative essay on the 400th anniversary of the Reformation, Lutheran pastor William Dallmann wrote,

> From justification by faith, it is an easy step to the universal priesthood of believers. The Old Testament distinction between priest and people, clergymen and laymen, is at an end. Christ, our high priest, has made all Christians priests unto God. All Christians are God's clergy, and so there is no special clerical order in the church. The ministry is an office, not an order, much less a threefold order of bishops, priests, deacons. . . . The church is a government of the people, by the people, and for the people, and all Christians are the people.[5]

This does not mean, as Robert McAfee Brown points out, that "everybody is his own priest, so that no community is necessary; but rather that everybody must be a priest to everybody else, so that community is a necessity."[6]

Thus the pastor, like Christ, is the servant, the enabler of the people, not the judge and ruler like the Old Testament priest, and the people are the ministers. Isaiah, speaking to "my people," predicted a time when all "will be known as the priests of the Lord" (Is. 61:6 TEV). With the coming of Jesus, that time arrived. New

Testament believers knew it. They chattered about Christ wherever they went; they gossiped the Gospel. They were joyous and outgoing about their faith, even though it could mean imprisonment and death. No wonder Christianity spread!

How different it is in many churches today. Telling the good news, calling on the sick, visiting the unsaved is the responsibility solely of the pastor. An article in the *Lutheran Witness* a few years ago, suggesting that the people of the parish have these duties too, drew a violent reaction from some laymen who said in essence, "That's the pastor's job—not ours!"

Not so, if we follow the exmple of the early Christians who met for worship in their homes. As ministers like them, we are to share our worldly goods, not just give offerings. We are to talk *to* God and *about* God. We, God's people, are to be living stones, using our differing gifts to build up others. We are to be God's temple, for Jesus Christ by His death "has freed us from our sins and made us a kingdom of priests to serve His God and Father" (Rev. 1:5, 6 TEV).

In our role as priests, we too will make Jesus Christ our Lord always. In doing this, our gifts—women's too—may include even prophecy. Our Lord promises: "I will pour out My Spirit on everyone; your sons and daughters will proclaim My message; your old men will have dreams, and your young men will see visions. At that time I will pour out My Spirit even on servants, both men and women" (Joel 2:28, 29 TEV).

What a blessing and opportunity for women—and men! What a challenge! How great it is to be a Christian!

As a Christian, I have real importance, for the Lord

Himself died that I might live. As a Christian, I don't need to be jealous of others, to gossip or criticize others, or stoop to any demeaning method of elevating myself. God Himself has planned my role. In God's eyes, I am more precious than jewels or gems, more precious than the life of His Son. Through God, I have a vocation that matters, I am to serve His people and tell His Good News. In Christ, I am one with the Lord. Since Christ, I am a priest. Through Christ, I will live forever. What more could any women want?

Or, for that matter, what more could any man want? Why then do some men fear to see woman take a step forward or move into a new role? Why do women's talents diminish some men's self-confidence? Perhaps as women come to understand who woman is, these men will come to understand who man is—and the whole world will be better for it. Then identity will not depend on sex, but on God. Then importance will stem from being God's creation and His redeemed child. Then you can be you, and I can be me, and all of us, fully and freely, can be what God created us to be!

4

I Am a Woman

A woman who honors the Lord should be praised. Give her credit for all she does. She deserves the respect of everyone.

Prov. 31:30, 31 TEV

How hard it is to find a capable wife! She is worth far more than jewels! Her husband puts his confidence in her, and he will never be poor. As long as she lives, she does him good and never harm.

She keeps herself busy making wool and linen cloth. She brings home food from out-of-the-way places, as merchant ships do. She gets up before daylight to prepare food for her family and to tell her servant girls what to do.

She looks at land and buys it, and with money she has earned, she plants a vineyard. She is a hard worker, strong and industrious.

She knows the value of everything she makes, and works late into the night. She spins her own thread and weaves her own cloth. She is generous to the poor and needy. She doesn't worry when it snows, because her family has warm clothing. She makes bedspreads and wears clothes of fine purple linen.

Her husband is well known, one of the leading citizens.

She makes clothes and belts, and sells them to merchants.

She is strong and respected and not afraid of the future.

She speaks with a gentle wisdom. She is always busy and looks after her family's needs.

Her children show their appreciation, and her husband praises her.

Prov. 31:10-18 TEV

DESPITE WHAT current-day woman critics have to say about the Biblical image of women, the fact is that the Scriptures, taken in their entirety, present a high view of womanhood. With joy and thanksgiving, I and others of my sex can answer the "Who am I?" question in a third way by saying, "I'm a woman—and proud of it!"

The problem, in some instances, is that church curricula, religious art, and sermons rarely focus on any women of the Bible. The impression is often given that all the Bible says specifically to women is keep silent, don't teach, and submit to your husbands.

What an eye-opener it is to read just the gospels, looking for any mention of women. They are there in abundance, and in the Old Testament too, women who should be models for Christian living today.

But how often do we talk about them? Do we even know who they are? At one ladies' meeting, the women were divided into two groups for a contest. One side was to name women of the Bible, and the other side was to name men of the Bible. Because the counselor was afraid that even women would not be familiar with many Biblical women, he provided that side with a list of the good women of Scripture. With the aid of his list, that side won!

And, how often do we picture women in congregational art? When a religious convention was meeting in a midwestern city, one of the special events was a church tour. The tour included a Protestant cathedral with many stained-glass windows portraying Old Testament heroes. As the guide identified the subjects, a young Episcopalian priest poked the lady next to him. "Where are the women?" he asked with a concerned smile. There were none.

The women *are* there though in the Bible. God worked through women. He revealed Himself directly to women (Eve, Sarah, and Hagar). He chose women to lead and inspire His people. He enabled them to influence men. Strong and capable—that's the most obvious way to describe some whose achievements are noted in the Old Testament, women like:

—*Deborah,* prophetess, judge, and ruler (appointed by God to this role, even though she was a married woman). Victimized by Canaanite cruelty and violence for 20 years, the people of Israel cried out to the Lord for help. In answer, God sent the courageous and forceful Deborah, who had been serving as a judge. She rallied Barak, who agreed to lead 10,000 men against the huge Canaanite army, with its 900 iron chariots, *only* if Deborah would go with him. God gave them the victory and there was peace in the land for the 40 years of Deborah's reign. The poetry of Judges 5, celebrating her success, says she "came like a mother for Israel."

—*Jael,* killer of the Canaanite army commander, Sisera. Many might disagree with the Bible's statement that Jael is "most fortunate of women," for her fame rests on taking a hammer and tent peg and killing Sisera by driving the peg through the side of his head and into the ground (Judges 4 and 5). However, her deed ended the rule of the Canaanites over Israel and was decreed by God so the somewhat timid Barak would not get sole credit for the conquest.

—*Jochebed,* mother of Moses, Aaron, and Miriam. Women dominated the events at the birth of Moses and virtually revolted against Pharaoh's decree that all male Hebrew babies be killed. (The Hebrews had multiplied so greatly that the Pharaoh was afraid they would take over Egypt.) When Moses was born, Jochebed hid him for three months (that took skill!), then placed him in a basket in the crocodile-infested Nile (that took faith!). When the king's daughter discovered Moses, Miriam cleverly arranged for Jochebed to be his nurse, and eventually the princess adopted him.

—*Sarah,* the covenant name given by God to Sarai, wife of Abraham, mother of Isaac. When she was 90 years old, God said to Abraham, "I will bless her, and I will give you a son by her. I will bless her, and she will become the mother of nations, and there will be kings among her descendants." Thus through the birth of Isaac, she became the mother of the Hebrew nation. It is interesting to note that when Sarah asks Abraham to send Hagar and her son away, God tells Abraham, "Do whatever Sarah tells you" (Gen. 21:12).

—*Hagar,* Sarah's Egyptian servant girl and mother of Abraham's first son, Ishmael. Twice the Lord appeared to her in the wilderness, the first time to urge her to go back and be Sarah's slave and the second to provide water and sustenance. God's blessing: "You are going to have a son, and you will name him Ishmael (meaning

God hears)." He will have many children and "they will become a nation."

—*Abigail,* the wise wife of Nabal, the fool. After David had protected the flocks and servants of Nabal, Nabal refused to give David anything in appreciation. Angered, David set out to murder Nabal. When Abigail heard, she gathered gifts, without Nabal's knowledge, and went out to meet David. She asked forgiveness and skillfully urged David to accept her offerings so that "when the Lord has made you king of Israel, then you will not have to feel regret or remorse, sir, for having killed without cause or for having taken your own revenge." David praised God for her—but when Nabal heard, he died of a stroke. David then proposed marriage and she became his wife.

—*Sheerah,* constructor of cities. The daughter of Ephraim, she built the towns of Upper and Lower Beth-horon and Uzzen-sheerah. Also the *daughters of Shallum* helped rebuild the wall of Jerusalem (Neh. 3:12).

—*Miriam,* unmarried heroine, prophetess, and leader in an age when marriage was a consecrated ideal. "I sent Moses, Aaron, and Miriam to lead you," the Lord tells His people in Micah 6:4. She is best known for the victory song in which she led the women at the Red Sea. When she rejected Moses' leadership and rebelled against his second wife (a foreigner and most likely of a dark-skinned race), God punished Miriam with leprosy.

—*Rebecca,* Isaac's wife. Reaction to Rebecca is divided. Some remember her beauty and graciousness which led Abraham's servant to choose her as Isaac's wife. They praise her for the determination which she showed in obtaining the blessing for Jacob, the son God intended to receive it, and the skill she demonstrated in masterminding Jacob's escape. Others see her as conniving, domineering, and treacherous, a mother who played favorites, a woman who tricked her husband.

—*Rachel,* the woman whom Jacob worked 14 years to earn. That fact places a high value on the wifely role. As the mother of Jospeh and Benjamin, she was the mother of two of the tribes of Israel—and the first recorded women in the Bible to die in childbirth.

—*Manoah's wife,* mother of Samson. Frightened after the angel of the Lord appeared to them, Manoah said, "We are sure to die, because we have seen God!" His wife, more wisely, disagreed, "If the Lord had wanted to kill us, he would not have accepted our offerings; he would not have shown us all this or told us such things at this time."

—*Naaman's servant girl,* a maid who shared her faith. Though a captive, she encouraged her master to go to the prophet in Samaria so he could be cured of his disease. A powerful witness!

—*Achsah,* the woman who asked for more. As freely as Achsah went to her father, so we should be able to go to our Lord in heaven to ask for a blessing. Because the land Caleb gave her as a dowry was dry, she then went to him and asked for springs—and he granted her request.

—*Hannah,* prophetess and devout mother of Samuel. When her prayer for a son was answered, she dedicated him to the Lord, taking him to the temple to serve at age three.

—*Vashti,* a modest woman of principles. When Ahasuerus wanted to exhibit Queen Vashti's beauty to his drunken dinner guests, she refused and the king divorced her.

—*Huldah,* respected prophetess. It was Huldah, not her husband and not the prophet Jeremiah, whom Josiah consulted when the Book of the Law was found in the House of the Lord. When she prophesied national ruin, Josiah instituted reforms, and a spiritual renewal resulted. A brilliant woman, historians believe she taught school in Jerusalem.

—*Widow of Zarephath,* a woman who learned to trust. With only a bit of flour and olive oil left in her home, the widow was about to prepare her last meal for herself and her son. Then seh expected to starve to death. When asked to share with Elijah, she did as told, and her bowl never ran out of flour, nor her jar out of oil. When her son died later, Elijah prayed and the boy was restored to life. Said the widow, "Now I know that you are a man of God and that the Lord really speaks through you!"

Two books of the Bible are named for women—Ruth and Esther. Through charm and persuasion, the courageous Esther saved the Jewish people from annihilation in Persia. The loyal Ruth insisted on staying with Naomi, her mother-in-law, after both were widowed. Later as the wife of Boaz, this Gentile became an ancestress of Christ.

From the four Old Testament women listed in the lineage of Jesus, we learn something of the inclusiveness and forgiveness of our Lord. Besides Ruth, there were Rahab, a prostitute who saved the lives of two of Joshua's spies by hiding them and then helping them escape; Bathsheba, the adulteress; and Tamar, an unwed mother. Because these women received the grace of God we can be reassured of the Lord's love for all of us sinners.

Many more Old Testament women could be mentioned, including, as could be said of some Old Testament men, a number of questionable character. One thing is sure—even in Old Testament days, the women did not necessarily remain in the background, despite the customs of their time, and the Lord did not reprimand them for this. In fact, He appeared to some, blessed many, and used them in guiding His people.

Most of these women are typified by the description in Proverbs 31. Over the centuries, this ideal woman has been portrayed by commentators as primarily a housewife. Her qualities and interests, however, extend far beyond her household and she seemingly could provide a pattern for women of today who are employed outside the home. She is strong and industrious. She earns money and uses it to plant a vineyard. She sells clothes and belts to merchants. She buys land. She speaks with wisdom. She is generous to the poor and needy—and she takes good care of her family. She's a busy woman!

* * *

Once Christ came, it was an even brighter world for women, not only because He is the Savior, but because He opened new doors for them, offered new equalities. So great were the opportunities He gave and so well did the woman take advantage of them that Libanius, a pagan teacher in Greece, commented, "What women these Christians have!"

Of particular importance is the fact that He encouraged women to learn. He permitted women to follow Him about the countryside—a radical act in itself since women were to be sheltered, protected, and veiled—and He taught them along with the men. His female followers included "women who had been healed of evil spirits and diseases: Mary (who was called Magdalene), from whom seven demons had been driven out; Joanna, whose husband Chuza was an officer in Herod's court; and Susanna, and many other women who used their own resources to help Jesus and his disciples" (Luke 8:2, 3 TEV). Women were in the crowds when He fed the 5,000 and 4,000.

In praising Mary for sitting at His feet and learning, He opened to women the study of the Scriptures, an activity previously limited to men. Only men then studied with the scribes. Only men gathered for philosophical discussions at the gates of the cities and in places of business and trade.

Rosemary Reuther calls the Mary and Martha incident the "keystone to the changed status of women." She notes,

> In a typical Jewish setting of that time women would not have been allowed to sit at the feet of a rabbi. With a few rare exceptions of rabbis' daughters, it was not considered worthwhile to waste time educating young women. Martha, irritated by her sister's behavior, asks Jesus to reprimand her. But to Martha's surprise Jesus comes to Mary's aid and rebukes Martha instead, saying, "Mary has chosen the good portion which shall not be taken away from her."
>
> Luke 10:42 RSV[7]

Jesus commissioned women to "go and tell." He also put His stamp of approval on their acts of worship.

While Jesus was eating, Mary of Bethany poured an

alabaster jar of very expensive perfume on His head. Criticizing the waste, the disciples said the perfume should have been sold and the money given to the poor. But Jesus said to them,

> Why are you bothering this woman? It is a fine and beautiful thing that she has done for Me. You will always have the poor people with you, but you will not always have Me. What she did was to pour this perfume on My body to get Me ready for burial. Now, I assure you that wherever this Gospel is preached all over the world, what she has done will be told in memory of her.
>
> Matt. 26:10-13 TEV

Even the ministrations of the woman who had led the sinful life were welcomed. While He was eating at the home of a Pharisee who had not given Him the customary kiss of welcome, nor provided water to wash His feet (also a custom in that dry climate), a woman approached. She washed His feet with her tears, dried them with her hair, kissed His feet, and poured perfume on them. Christ commended her love and saw it as proof that she had been forgiven much. "Whoever has been forgiven little shows only a little love" (Luke 7:47 TEV).

After Christ's death, faithful women remained at Calvary and followed the men to the tomb where they were the first to learn from the angel that He was risen, the first to see Christ, and the first to be told to "Go and tell." To this day, women should realize what a great commission is theirs from the Lord!

In His teachings, Christ uses the experiences of women as well as men. Jesus compares God to the woman who lost the coin. Jesus also compares the kingdom of God with a woman mixing a batch of dough. In His parable of the coming judgment, He says, "two women will be at a mill grinding meal; one will be taken away, the other will be left behind." (Matt. 24:41 TEV). In His parable of the 10 virgins, five are prepared and enter the wedding feast; the unprepared five are left behind. The value of continued prayer is taught in His parable of the widow and the judge. When the woman keeps coming to the judge and pleading her rights, He finally grants her request "because of all the trouble this widow is giving me."

To illustrate the fact that a prophet is never welcome in his own hometown, Jesus refers to Elijah going to the widow of Zarephath in Sidon, rather than to widows in Israel. When the people ask for a miracle, Christ refuses and predicts: "On the judgment day the Queen of Sheba will stand up and accuse the people of today, because she traveled all the way from her country to listen to King Solomon's wise teaching; and there is something here, I tell you, greater than Solomon."

As Jesus speaks of His coming death and resurrection, He compares the reaction of His followers to a woman about to give birth:

> She is sad because her hour of suffering has come; but when the baby is born, she forgets her suffering, because she is happy that a baby has been born into the world. That is how it is with you: now you are sad but I will see you again, and your hearts will be filled with gladness, the kind of gladness that no one can take away from you.
>
> John 16:21-22 TEV

Jesus performed miracles for women as well as men. He healed Simon's mother-in-law of her fever. He healed the 12-year-old daughter of Jairus. He praised the Canaanite woman for her faith and healed her daughter. He raised the widow's son. One Sabbath day He healed a woman who had been crippled for 18 years.

At first glance, the public search which Christ made for the woman who had touched Him in the crowd may seem cruel. She had suffered a "flow of blood" for 12 years and spent all her money going to doctors to no avail. Now she had touched Christ in faith and was healed. But He didn't let it end there. "Who touched my clothes?" He asked. Finally the woman came forward, trembling with fear. She knelt at His feet and told Him the whole truth. His response: "Go in peace, and be healed of your trouble."

What did it mean? In this action, Christ rejected all the Old Testament taboos and rituals associated with uncleanness due to blood and menstruation. Under those laws, a woman menstruating was unclean for seven days and anyone who touched her was unclean until evening. Whatever she sat or lay on was unclean. If her husband had intercourse with her, he and any bed on which he slept were contaminated for seven days. The same rules applied to any other flow of blood and required that a ritual of purification be performed at the temple when the flow stopped.

Thus, under these laws, Christ became unclean when the woman touched Him. He deliberately sought her out to end that ordinance for all time.

Jesus supported the sanctity of marriage and the family. When questioned about divorce, He repeated God's statement that "a man will leave his father and mother and unite with his wife, and the two will become one. So they are no longer two, but one. Man must not separate , then, what God has joined together" (Matt. 19:5, 6 TEV). "If a man divorces his wife . . . he is guilty of making her commit adultery if she marries again; and the man who marries her commits adultery also" (Matt. 5:32 TEV).

Yet Christ was quick to emphasize that we all need forgiveness. When the adulteress was brought before him to be stoned (one wonders where the man was who had been caught with her in the act), Christ's answer was, "Let him who is without sin among you cast the first stone."

"Respect your father and your mother," Christ also tells His followers, but He is quick to place all human relationships in their proper perspective. At age 12, Christ remained in the temple when His family returned home after the Passover festival. As an adult, when his mother and brothers tried to speak with Him while He was addressing the teachers and Pharisees, Jesus answered, "'Who is My mother? Who are My brothers?' Then He pointed to His disciples and said, 'Look! Here are My mother and My brothers! Whoever does what My Father in heaven wants him to do is My brother, My sister, and My mother'" (Matt. 12:48-50 TEV).

Further guidance for women—and men—can be found in the lives of some of the outstanding New Testament women.

One of the first recorded missionaries, and the first person to whom Christ revealed that He is the Messiah, was the Samaritan woman at the well. The fact that Christ would talk to a strange woman, and a Samaritan at that, was a shock to the disciples. Not only did He ask her for a drink (Jews did not use the same cups and bowls that Samaritans used), but He told her of the living water. When she expressed her belief in a coming Messiah, Christ said, "I am He, I who am talking with you." She went back to town and told all the people. They came to see Him, begged Him to stay with them, and many believed. That's what evangelism is, bringing people to see Jesus—and this Samaritan proved women can do it too.

A greater example of trust one can never find than that of the Virgin Mary, particularly when you think of what she must have gone through. It is so easy for us today to think only of the beautiful baby born to her and forget the setting in which this took place.

Imagine for a moment what it was like for Mary. In a country where an adulteress is stoned to death, an angel tells her that she will give birth to a child. "I am a virgin. How, then, can this be?" she asks. The angel explains, and Mary says, "I am the Lord's servant; may it happen to me as you have said (Luke 1:34, 38 TEV)." Her beautiful Magnificat is sung in worship services to this day.

When Joseph, her fiance, discovers she is pregnant, he plans to break the engagement and put her away privately. An angel appears to him, saying, "Do not be afraid to take Mary to be your wife. For it is by the Holy Spirit that she has conceived. She will have a son, and you will name Him Jesus, because He will save His people from their sins" (Matt. 1:20, 21 TEV).

Joseph does as he is told, but no angel tells the neighbors and friends. Can you imagine what they must have thought and said? What would you think if a Jewish girl down the street told you today that she is pregnant by the Holy Spirit? And then there is the journey to Bethlehem, on a donkey, when Mary is "heavy with child." What women today would want to endure such a trip, but Mary does not complain.

When they get to Bethlehem, there is no place for them to stay—despite the census, a most abnormal situation! Bethlehem was Joseph's home town (Luke 2:2). Most likely he had relatives there, and Hebrew hospitality decreed that relatives, even very distant ones, were always welcomed into one's home. Perhaps Joseph was being ostracized because he had not followed the law in regard to Mary. Some scholars also suspect that the innkeeper may not have wanted a pregnant woman in the inn because giving birth would cause the room to be unclean.

Whatever the case, prophecy was fulfilled and Jesus was born in lowly surroundings—a stable. How we glamorize that setting in Christmas pageants! Compare it for a moment with today's antiseptic hospital delivery rooms—and think of Mary, giving birth to the Savior of the world in a stable, surrounded by animals. Think of Christ being born in such a place. How we should praise our Lord for the humiliation He was willing to endure from the very beginning for our sakes! How grateful we should be too for Mary's example of trust and devotion. Through Eve, sin came into the world; through Mary, the Savior was born.

Another example of faith is found in Martha. We often condemn her because she chose to work in the kitchen when Christ visited. Yet there is no more beautiful confession of faith than hers in John 11.

> Martha said to Jesus, "If you had been here, Lord, my brother would not have died! But I know that even now God will give You whatever You ask Him for." "You brother will rise to life," Jesus told her. "I

> know," she replied, "that he will rise to life on the last day." Jesus said to her, "I am the Resurrection and the Life. Whoever believes in Me will live, even though he dies; and whoever lives and believes in Me will never die. Do you believe this?" "Yes, Lord!" she answered. "I do believe that You are the Messiah, the Son of God, who was to come into the world."
>
> John 11:21-27 TEV

The New Testament also has its prophetesses. Although Anna was 88 years old, this widow never left the temple. "Day and night she worshiped God, fasting and praying." When Mary and Joseph brought the baby Jesus to the temple to present him to the Lord, both Simeon and the prophetess Anna proclaimed that He was the fulfillment of all God's promises. Both thanked the Lord that they had lived long enough to see the Savior. Then Anna spoke about Christ to all who were waiting for God to set Jerusalem free, a fact which has led one author to call her the first Christian missionary.[8] The other prophetesses mentioned in the New Testament are the four daughters of Philip the evangelist, at whose home Paul stayed.

Other women not to be forgotten are:

—*Eunice,* Timothy's mother. Married to a non-Jewish husband, this Jewish woman and her mother, Lois, taught Timothy the Scriptures from little on. She was probably converted to Christ at the time of Paul's first trip through Asia Minor.

—*Priscilla,* the teacher and tent maker. She and her husband Aquila accompanied Paul on some of his trips and risked their lives for him. A church met in their house. In five of the six passages where the pair are mentioned, contrary to Jewish custom, Priscilla's name precedes that of Aquila. It is believed therefore that she was the more fluent and learned. She and Aquila took Apollos, the brilliant teacher and convert, aside after he spoke in the synagog and "explained to him more correctly the Way of God." Tertullian, a prominent author of that day, wrote, "By the holy Prisca, the Gospel is preached." In the Catacomb of Priscilla in Rome is a fresco depicting women breaking bread and celebrating Holy Communion.

—*Dorcas, seamstress and servant of the poor.* "She spent all her time doing good and helping the poor," says the Bible. When she died, all the widows cried and showed Peter the shirts and coats Dorcas had made for them. Peter, in the first raising of the dead after the Ascension of Christ, turns to her body and says, "Tabitha, get up!" She opened her eyes and sat up. The news spread and many people believed.

—*Lydia,* Paul's first European convert. The New Testament's best-known businesswoman, Lydia was a seller of purple. Called to Macedonia (a Roman colony) in a dream, Paul immediately left by ship. That Sunday as he went to the riverside where he thought the Jews would be gathered for prayer, he found a group of women. He talked to them and Lydia was converted, and she and all the people of her household were baptized.

When Paul moved on to Berea, the people "listened to the message with great eagerness, and every day they studied the Scriptures to see if what Paul said was really true. Many of them believed; and many Greek women of high social standing and many Greek men also believe" (Acts 17:11-12 TEV). What an example for congregations today!

—*Phoebe,* church officer at Cenchrae. Paul gives two titles to Phoebe—*diakonos* and *prostatis.* In his writings, Paul uses *diakonos* 22 times. In English versions, it is translated 18 times as minister, three times as deacon, and only once—in relation to Phoebe—as servant. (Some of the very newest versions now use deaconess or church officer.) There can be only one reason the translators did not choose minister in this 22d instance, says Russell Prohl, and that is because Phoebe was a woman. "Diakonos is a title which Paul applies to himself and to Tychicus, Epaphras, Timothy, and Apollos, all full-fledged pastors, preachers, and evangelists. According to the title Phoebe may have had all of these offices."[9]

The second title, *prostatis,* also indicates authority. Says Prohl: "The Greek word means 'one who presides,' 'the chief of a party,' 'a president,' 'ruler,' 'foreman,' 'superintendent.'"[10] Whenever Paul uses the verb form of this noun, translators always give it the meaning of "rule." Why then for her is the word translated "helper"? The New Jerusalem Bible comes closer to the original meaning with its statement: "She has looked after a great many people, myself included." Here at least the sense of organizer or arranger, chairman or responsible party comes through.

Evidently Paul assumes Phoebe will continue with her work while she is in Rome, for he directs the congregation, "Assist her in whatsoever business she hath need of you," or in the words of Phillips, "Give her any assistance with her work that she may need."

Prohl believes that Phoebe, before her conversion, may have been one of the women philosophers of Athens. "She would then be above the law, permitted to travel freely, and to preach to men as well as women."[11] Tradition has it that she carried Paul's "Letter to the Romans" to Rome.

Paul also speaks of many other women who were "co-laborers" with him. Space does not permit identifying all the women with positive images in Scripture. Suffice it to say that all who merit mention were women of achievement. They are there because of their deeds, their faith, their devotion. They were an important part of the Hebrew and Christian communities—and so it should be for the women of the church today.

5

I Am Married I Am Single

Submit yourselves to one another because of your reverence for Christ.

Wives, submit yourselves to your husbands as to the Lord. For the husband has authority over his wife just as Christ has authority over the church; and Christ is Himself the Savior of the church, His body. And so wives must submit themselves completely to their husbands just as the church submits itself to Christ.

Husbands, love your wives just as Christ loved the church and gave His life for it. . . . Men ought to love their wives just as they love their own bodies. A man who loves his wife loves himself. (No one ever hates his own body. Instead, he feeds it and takes care of it, just as Christ does the church; for we are members of His body.) As the Scripture says, 'For this reason a man will leave his father and mother and unite with his wife, and the two will become one.' There is a deep secret truth revealed in this Scripture, which I understand as applying to Christ and the church. But it also applies to you; every husband must love his wife as himself, and every wife must respect her husband.

Eph. 5:21-25, 28-33 TEV

WHEN WE GET beyond the point of understanding who we are in terms of being God's creation, a Christian and a woman, chances are most of us have many and varied answers: I'm a wife, a mother, a daughter. I'm single. I'm a musician, deaconess, secretary, writer, physicist, production line worker, waitress, teacher, nurse, student, homemaker.

There's no end to the list or to the Christian implications of each role. The most obvious: Whoever wants to be great must be the servant of the rest (Mark 9:35); do unto others as you would have them do unto you; love your neighbor as yourself. When it comes to marriage, however, the Bible gets more specific.

How grateful Christian women should be for the modern translations of the Bible, particularly for Ephesians 5:21: "Submit yourselves *to one another* because of your reverence for Christ" (TEV). In the King James version, that verse is simply a phrase attached to the preceding section. In all the new translations, that verse is the topic sentence for the entire section which follows on Christian marriage.

Marriage thus requires a dual submission. The wife is to honor and respect her husband, for he is in authority. That's necessary, for in any relationship between two people there are going to be times of disagreement. Someone has to make the final decision after all possibilities have been weighed, if the couple cannot agree. God says the husband has that role.

But the submission of marriage is a two-way street, for the directive doesn't stop there (although too often that's the impression given in some churches). Husbands are told to love their wives as Christ loved the church "and gave Himself for it." Christ gave His life! What woman could refrain from honoring a man who is willing to give his life for her, who loves her as he loves himself and treats her accordingly, who strives to imitate our just and compassionate God?

There's none of the old German "Herr Papa" picture here, none of the table-thumping "I am the lord and master" image, none of the demanding "Do as I say, my word is law" directive. No, the Biblical perspective offers a marriage where two people really are one, where the husband is a loving leader and the wife a respectful co-partner. (When I made these statements in one speech, a woman took me aside afterwards and said, "Why do you restrict your remarks to the German papa? The Norwegians had them too!" Most likely she's right, for I suspect the pompous patriarch can be found in most nationalities.)

One pastor says the Ephesians portrayal of marriage strikes fear in his heart, for he knows that he can never live up to this Biblical expectation. Only Christ could so totally and so willingly give Himself for others.

Nevertheless, it's a worthy goal for men, and what a witness for the church. When married couples conduct their lives accordingly, their relationship demonstrates to everyone what Christianity is all about. The foundation of the Christian faith is a loving God who gave His life for His people, and the people in response love and honor their God.

Once we understand this, and recognize the uneducated status which women had in Bible times, we can better understand some of Paul's other directives to women and the importance of those directives in preserving marriage. In regard to women, Paul simply is not the ogre that some modernists make him out to be. There were practical reasons for the directives Paul was inspired by God to give. God's law is always that of order, not confusion.

But confusion is what Paul found in the Corinthian congregation and so he writes to solve the problem. He lays down some procedures: Only one person is to speak at a time; when someone speaks in a tongue, there is to be an interpreter; to preserve the marriage ideal, the wife is to be quiet in the public service.

As has been pointed out, women of the early church were definitely uneducated. The Missouri Synod Commission on Theology and Church Relations (CTCR) made note of this in its study on *Woman Suffrage in the Church:*

> In the Judaism of the first century even learning, going to school, was a right denied to women. To have insisted on the kind of opportunity for learning which was available to Jewish boys and men would have been considered an act of impudence. Woman's lot was to pursue her task in quietness and subordination.[12]

Thus the statement in 1 Cor. 14:35 TEV was totally appropriate: "If they [women] want to find out something, they should ask their husbands." Their questions most likely would have been disruptive, and since a wife was not to speak in public, her interruption of the reader, the teacher or the prophet (or prophetess) would have demeaned her husband and jeopardized her marriage. Speaking in public was grounds for divorce.[13]

So was appearing in public with her head uncovered. The Greek veil or the Hebrew head cloth were required apparel for wives. To appear otherwise would identify a woman as a Corinthian prostitute. Unveiled, the wife was in effect renouncing her marriage. "If her husband was a pious Jew, he was expected to divorce her. If he was a pagan, he could lock her out of her home without explanation," says Prohl.[14]

Thus a woman's service in the church and her freedom in Christ does not set aside her relationship to her husband. But, with her head covered, she could lead prayers and prophesy during gatherings and services of the believers, according to 1 Cor. 11:2-16. The Commission on Theology and Church Relations (p. 8) agrees: "A distinction is made between the prophetesses of chapter 11 and women who are present at worship as ordinary members of a congregation. While the former may speak, if properly attired, the latter are to remain silent."

Paul explains in Titus 2:5 why the women must submit themselves to their husbands and be self-controlled and pure. It is "so that no one will speak evil of the message that comes from God."

Because of the Christians' agape (love) feasts, their common concern for the widows and the poor in their midst, their holding of property in common, the gossips were saying that Christians were also sharing their wives in common. To prevent the rumors from continuing, the apostles, while recognizing the interdependence of women and men (1 Cor. 11:11, 12), decreed that women should not ask questions or interrupt during the congregation's public gatherings. Rather they were to learn in silence, giving all due respect to their husbands.

Today the headcovering no longer signifies marriage in the eyes of the world, so the church has dropped that restriction. To some degree, the regulation of total silence, which no longer applies in the world, is likewise gradually disappearing in the church. Most Protestant denominations permit women to speak and vote in congregational gatherings, realizing that the authority of the parish rests not in an individual or a sex, but in the Christian community, the royal priesthood which includes all believers.

The principles which Paul followed and which still apply today are: 1) God's ordiances, including those related to marriage, are not to be violated, and 2) the actions or customs of the church are not to be so alien to the culture, so strange or different that these peculiarities prevent people from coming to know Christ. An example of such a peculiarity today would be the costumes and buggies of the Amish. Thus it is a blessing that in this century most Protestant churches have approved the organization of women's societies and adopted woman suffrage. These decisions removed barriers to the Gospel in a world where women have these freedoms.

Speaking of marriage brings to mind the beautiful black Rhodesian woman who attended the Lausanne Evangelism Congress. Over lunch one day she told how she is working through her church and the YWCA to change the marriage pattern of her country to the single family unit customary in the United States.

"When girls marry in our country, their mothers cry—and for good reason," she explained. "The bride becomes a part of her husband's family, a slave to her in-laws. She must do as they say. She has no life of her own. In your country, the two establish their own household; they are one. That is so much better."

As she spoke, I could not help thinking of all the

articles in American magazines about the impossibility of a lifelong union . . . articles advocating communal living, wife-swapping, and serial matrimony (one divorce after another, with each marriage a new episode). Today 1.3 million men and women live together without being married because they are not ready to make a complete commitment to one another.

Such arrangements miss one of the beautiful experiences of this life—the God-blessed union of two who become one, the support of a person who loves you totally and is dedicated to your welfare, someone who will never leave you until death parts you. When conducted in obedience to the Lord's precepts, a Christian marriage enables and encourages both partners to grow in Christ, to use their talents to the fullest of their God-given potential, and to share with the world a model of God's relationship with His people.

* * *

Because women have so many freedoms today, single women also have greater opportunity to serve the Lord. Singleness can offer exciting Christian challenges and a blessed role.

Now that women are free to establish their own homes, single persons can make that home just as much a center of Christian hospitality as the home of a married couple. They can host Christian gatherings and Bible study groups. They can sew, serve, garden, write, teach, pray, study—all to the glory of God and the benefit of the Christian community. They can care for the sick, the needy, the orphans. They can welcome widows. They can lend the listening ear so needed in this fast-paced world.

Moreover, they can enjoy an independence never before possible for singles. They can travel, try different job options, and make their own decisions without having to coordinate or change their plans to fit in with the desires of others in the household. They can concentrate on the course God has outlined for them, without having to detour to avoid conflict with others in the home.

They can pursue their special interests—and still be a resource to others. One single friend of mine always attends religious meetings on the home and family. Says she: "So often when my friends have problems in their marriages or family life, they call me. They want an impartial view—and I want to be prepared."

At the Lausanne Congress on Evangelization, several sessions were held on evangelism among women. Much was said about the role of wives. Finally one lady commented, "Enough of this—now give us some guidance for single women." The moderator called on Miss Jean Raddon of Australia, a leader of women's retreats across that continent. Her advice: Remember that our God is a great God. If He hasn't given you a husband, it is because He has some other good in mind for you. Therefore: 1) Seek His willf or yoru life, 2) Discover your spiritual gifts, your talents, and use them in His service, and 3) As for a husband, keep looking but not longing!

* * *

Single or married, employed and/or homemaker, all women share a basic identity as God's creation and His redeemed children. That fact, however, has rarely been apparent in the treatment of women throughout the centuries, as we shall see from a look at history.

6

Woman, A Necessary Evil?

Woman is a pitfall—a pitfall, an hole, a ditch.

Anonymous Mesopotamian poet

There is no evil so terrible as woman.

A woman should be good for everything at home, but for nothing away from it.

Euripides, about 400 B.C.

Men must have mothers, and so women are a necessary evil.

Confucius

Clever men build cities,
Clever women topple them.
. . . Women have long tongues,
Stairways to ruin.
Disorder is not sent down from Heaven
But bred by these women.

Confucius

Bitter indeed it is to be born a woman,
It is difficult to imagine anything so low.

Fu Hsuan, 3d Century

Among all savage beasts, none is found so harmful as woman.

John Chrysostom

Woman are almost all timid by nature, soft, slow, and therefore more useful when they sit still and watch over our things.

Leon Battista, 15th century

The whole education of women ought to be relative to men. To please them, to be useful to them, to care for them, and to make life sweet and agreeable to them. These duties of women should be taught them from their infancy.

—Jean Jacques Rousseau, 18th century

Describing how he decided the fitness of a political candidate, William Shakespeare said, "I have no other but a woman's reason: I think him so, because I think him so."

Woman's world is her husband, her family, her children and her home. We do not find it right when she presses into the world of man.

Adolph Hitler

OBVIOUSLY THE QUESTION of woman's role has been around for ages!

Even one of the first females in early mythology, Babylon's moon goddess Ishtar (alias Inanna, the Sumerian goddess of war and love), complained in a poem, "Me, the woman, why did you treat differently? Me, the holy Inanna, where are my powers?"

To better understand today's questioning women and the women's movement as a whole, and to better appreciate the freedoms which Biblical women enjoyed, particularly in the New Testament, we need to review the attitudes toward women in the cultures which surrounded God's people in earliest times. How, for instance, did the women of Mesopotamia, Egypt, Greece, and Rome answer the question, "Who am I?"

In Mesopotamia the answer was simple: "We're second class citizens. We're drudges. We have little power or choice. Our chief purpose is procreation and pleasure for men."

Thus these women were mere property, owned first by their fathers and then their husbands. While men could have numerous wives or concubines, a married woman could be killed or mutilated for adultery. The crime was not one of morality but one against the husband's property.

Occupations for unmarried women were limited to priestess, prostitute, ale-wife (wineseller), and slave. The mark of the married woman was her veil, which she always wore outside her home.

Although the wives of kings were simply called "she of the palace" rather than queen, the achievements of at least one king's wife, Semiramis, are recorded in history. When her husband died, she ruled until her son was old enough to take over. During that period she enlarged Babylon, built the hanging gardens, and enclosed the city with a wall 42 miles long and wide enough for six chariots to travel side by side. Quite an accomplishment for a woman of that day!

In this culture, and in most primitive cultures with their many deities, the sun and sun gods represented masculinity and work and achievement. The phases of the moon, on the other hand, were equated with menstruation (the word means "moon change"), and its cyclic growth was compared with the swelling of pregnancy. Thus the moon goddess became the source of fertility, leading to the fertility cults and sacred prostitution—and the sexual orgies of the society which Abraham left in religious protest.

In Egypt, by contrast, women could sue and testify in court, as well as own, buy, and sell property. This gained them another "privilege"—paying taxes.

As in Mesopotamia, women exercised greater power as mothers than as wives. The queens were the exception. They were considered consorts of god (the king). Although their pyramids were smaller than those of the kings, they were permitted tombs of equal size.

Several women were elevated to the throne, including the beautiful Nefertiti and the conniving and powerful Cleopatra. Best known among the very early queens was Hatshepsut, who restored peace to the land and ruled as *king,* probably, according to Vern L. Bullough, because "the titles, laudatory inscriptions, and ceremonies were all designed for men and were so deeply rooted in tradition and dogma that it was easier for a woman to adapt herself to fit the titles than to change the titles to fit her sex."[15]

Just as the Jews often contended with the pagan gods of their Mediterranean neighbors, so the early Christians contended with the power of Rome and the culture of Greece. Mention Greece and we think of its love of literature and learning, its interest in history and science and philosophy, its lofty ideals and sophisticated intellectualism.

Yet its treatment of women differed little from other cultures. Although Grecian women at the time of Homer apparently enjoyed a near balance of roles, the patriarchal system soon took over, with the eldest male in the family serving as absolute head. Unwanted girl babies and crippled male infants were put to death to keep a balance in population.

Because the Greeks believed that everything is

placed here for a single function, women were assigned a very narrow role. Demosthenes explained:

> Hetaerae (mistress/companions) we keep for the sake of pleasure; concubines (female slaves) for the daily care of our persons; wives to bear us legitimate children and to be the trusted guardians of our households.[16]

Though they may have been trusted guardians, wives were not included in social events and had no legal rights. The male's contempt for woman is typified by the god Zeus, who mated with almost every female deity (each of whom had her own single function—chastity, sexual love, faithfulness, and fertility). That same contempt and the claim that women are the cause of every evil in this world are personified by the story of Pandora.

Angered because Prometheus had stolen fire from heaven, Zeus ordered an evil being created whom all men would desire. The result, according to this legend, was the first woman, the beautiful and talented Pandora, whom the gods gave to the brother of Prometheus. With her she brought a box which she was never to open—but curiosity soon won, and out came all the sins, diseases, and troubles which plague mankind. Quickly she closed the lid, but later opened it once more to allow hope (which was stuck under the cover) to go free.

Probably the most renowned representatives of Greek thought were Plato and Aristotle. Women fared no better with them. Although women in the "Republic," Plato's ideal state, were given the right to education and a public life, marriage was advocated as temporary, with land, houses, wives, and family to be held communally.

Aristotle believed that all females, both animal and human, were inferior to males. The value of women, he said, was their beautiful body and love of work—but in silence was their glory.

Far greater freedom and dignity were accorded Roman wives and mothers. They could go out of their houses unveiled to shop, visit the baths, see their friends, worship at the temples, and engage in business. At one period in history they were even permitted to sit with men at the amphitheater. Some husbands gave their wives beautiful adornments and expensive gifts, enabling them to become wealthy in their own name.

As a result the Oppian law had to be repealed. Passed in 215 B.C., it forbade women to wear ornaments or multicolored dresses and ride in chariots. The repeal came in 195 B.C. after women demonstrated in the streets. This commotion caused Cato to comment:

> If every married man had been concerned to ensure that his own wife looked up to him and respected his rightful position as her husband, we should not have half this trouble with women *en masse*. Instead, women have become so powerful that our independence has been lost in our own homes and is now being trampled and stamped underfoot in public. We have failed to restrain them as individuals, and now they have combined to reduce us to our present panic . . . Woman is a violent and uncontrolled animal and it is no good giving her the reins and expecting her not to kick over the traces . . . What they want is complete freedom, or, not to mince words, license . . . Suppose you allow them to acquire or extort one right after

another, and in the end to achieve complete equality with men, do you think that you will find them bearable? Nonsense. Once they have achieved equality, they will be your masters.[17]

Neither the education of Greece nor the demonstrations of Roman women, however, succeeded in freeing women from the roles of prostitute, pagan priestess, procreator, and pleasure-provider to man—the roles decreed for them in early civilizations. And even the influence of the Bible and its concept of womanhood did not change that image for centuries.

With the split and demise of the Roman Empire in the 4th and 5th centuries, eastern women in the Byzantine empire benefited from Christian concepts which permitted them to be active in society by helping the poor and unfortunate. Nevertheless they had to be veiled in public and never dined with anyone but close friends and relatives, even in their own house. When new acquaintances of the husband or sons came for dinner, the women were secluded. Convents, however, offered single women a new opportunity for education and service.

The Muslims who made their way from Arabia across North Africa and into Spain by the 700s are credited with discoveries in medicine and mathemetics—yet they claimed it was a calamity to teach daughters to read and write. Marriage was seen as good, so good that men were encouraged to marry several wives—but a husband was required to treat all women in his harem equally. Daughters were permitted to inherit, but only half the amount of sons' inheritance.

During the Middle Ages in Europe, women tended

the home, the poultry, the dairy, the garden and helped the thatcher and the sheep-shearer. Husbands still had total control over their wives, except in the exercise of their religious duties. There the rules of the Lord and the rules of the church superceded the rule of the husband.

But the church, through its priests, also downgraded women. While practicing abstinence and celibacy as part of their marriage to the church, priests freely condemned women for their failure to match the virtues of the exalted Virgin Mary. Mary was perfect in the eyes of the church, and women in their humanity could only feel more inferior by contrast.

A 13th-century Franciscan cleric noted in his autobiography, "Lo, woman is the head of sin, a weapon of the devil, expulsion from Paradise, mother of guilt, corruption of the ancient law."[18] Small wonder that husbands were free to beat their wives!

From such accusations, it was a short step to the conclusion that women were witches. As the epidemic of witchcraft and witch-hunting fanned throughout Europe and America, it is estimated that 300,000 innocent women were tormented, tortured, and burned at the stake from 1484 to 1782.

To some extent, however, the age of chivalry and the beginning of courtly romance did place women in a new light. As knights and nobles set off on crusades and wars, poets wrote lyrics lauding the qualities of women. Moreover, the journeys of the male made the female important, for it was she who directed the servants and the estate during her husband's absence.

To this, Protestantism and the Reformation added the impetus to read. All Christians, men and women, were urged to "search the Scriptures"—and the printing press made copies available, not just to clerics and rulers, but also to the middle class. Schools opened for girls as well as boys, and books were written on the education of girls.

At last some men were bold enough to come to the defense of women—and in print! Erasmus, in his support of education for females, noted that "a girl cooped up with 'a foolish and empty-headed woman' was more likely to learn mischief than if she read good books."[19]

Women too began to write in their own defense. As previously noted, Marguerite de Navarre went so far as to say that "woman was the masterpiece of God since she was formed after man and was God's last work."[20] Ironically, those who complimented her on this stance commented that she "had a manly heart in a woman's body."[21]

Today historians commend women for their role in the French Revolution, the American Revolutionary War, and the Civil War, where women not only gave strong encouragement to the men who fought, but on occasion joined them in battle, sometimes disguised as men. History also praises the courage and fortitude of the Puritan women who endured such hardships in the new country and the pioneer women who helped settle the west.

They wove cloth, preserved food, fended off wild animals, and worked side by side with their husbands in farming, butchering, and trading.

Despite their hardiness, they were bracketed with children and apprentices when the laws of this land were written. As Thomas Jefferson said, "Were our

State a pure democracy there would still be excluded from our deliberations women who, to prevent deprivation of morals and ambiguity of issues, should not mix promiscuously in gatherings of men."

When the Declaration of Independence stated that "all men are created equal," it meant exactly that—*men*. A woman was expected to obey her husband or nearest of male kin. Marriage meant "civil death," notes the report of the U.S. National Commission on the Observance of International Women's Year. In marriage, "her person and her property would be owned by her husband—a concept rooted in English common law and brought to this country by the colonists." Ridicule, humiliation, and bitter opposition faced those women who dared to seek equal treatment for themselves.

Theoretically the Industrial Revolution should have resulted in a better life for women, but such was not the case. Instead it brought them into factories at substandard wages and over-standard hours. Before long, women were seeking new reforms—working conditions, suffrage, and temperance.

And now the goal of women reformers is "liberation"!

* * *

From Ishtar to Steinem, the questioning has gone on, the struggle has continued . . . the struggle of women to use their God-given abilities as they see them, not as men see them.

Yet the subjection has not held down all women. Though not as plentiful as men, the names of women do appear in secular history as outstanding (and sometimes notorious) rulers, writers, and pace-setters.

Besides Hatshepsut and Cleopatra in early times, they include: *Hypatia* (370—415), a philosopher in Alexandria; *Eudocia* (401—460), cofounder (with her husband) of the University of Constantinople; *Sappho,* a Greek poetess about 600 B.C., and *Theodora,* Byzantine empress (527—548) who preserved the crown for Justinian I.

Throughout the ages in Europe there were: *Anna Commena,* the first female historian; *Catherine the Great,* a German princess who became empress of Russia, built schools and hospitals, and promoted education for women; *Madame Curie,* the scientist who with her husband discovered radium; *Olympe de Gouges* (1745—93), the French dramatist who wrote "Declaration of Rights of Woman and Citizen"; *Christine de Pisan* (1363—1431), Italian poet and moralist whom some consider the first feminist and who with her writing supported three children; *Elizabeth I,* Queen of England during one of the most glorious periods in English history. Those who could not understand how a woman could be such an outstanding ruler decided she must be a man in disguise.

Also there were: *Joan of Arc,* "the deliverer of France"; *Florence Nightingale,* founder of the nursing profession as it is known today; *Mary, Queen of Scots,* last Roman Catholic ruler of Scotland, beheaded by Elizabeth 1; *Mary Wollstonecraft* (1759—97), founder of the movement for female emancipation in England and author of "Vindication of the Rights of Woman."

Mary I, Queen of England, crowned in 1553, tried to bring England back to the Roman Catholic Church. She was known as "Bloody Mary" because over 300 persons were burned at the stake during her reign.

Fanny Mendelssohn was said to be a better musician than her brother Felix but her family opposed public recognition of her works, some of which have recently been recorded.

Isabella, Queen of Spain, was one of few persons who saw merit in the ideas of Columbus. Her support of him gave Spain its first claim in America. With Ferdinand V, her husband, she built new roads, standardized coinage, and increased justice throughout the country.

Bouboulina and Manot Mavrogenous were two Grecian heroines who "manned" their own ship in the Revolution of 1821 and fought against the Turks. Compare this with the fact that in some traditional cultures, including Islam, women are not permitted to swim.

And then there were *Anne Bonney* and *Mary Read,* two English women who became full-fledged pirates, spending several years on pirate ships!

In American history there were: *Clara Barton,* founder and first president of the American Red Cross; *Ada Kepley,* the first woman to be graduated from an accredited school of law (Union College of Law in Chicago); *Myra Bradwell,* who, when kept from practicing law by the legal profession, instituted reforms through a legal periodical which she founded; and *Elizabeth Blackwell,* the first woman to complete a medical education in America, only to find that no hospital would hire a woman doctor. She solved that by founding a hospital for women and children in 1853. A medal in her honor is awarded to women physicians for achievements in medicine.

Sarah Hale, (1788—1879), the "first woman editor in America . . . made *Godey's Lady's Book* the forerunner of the modern women's magazine. She persuaded President Lincoln to adopt Thanksgiving as a national holiday, helped to organize Vassar College, advocated women as teachers in public schools, and instituted the country's first day nursery."[22]

Others in American history include: *Dorothea Dix,* crusader for the mentally ill, and superintendent of U.S. Army nurses during the Civil War; *Julia Ward Howe,* author of the "Battle Hymn of the Republic"; *Laura Keene,* actress and first woman to win success as a theater manager in the U.S. (she played the heroine at Ford's Theater the night Lincoln was shot); *Helen Keller,* blind and deaf author and lecturer, champion of the blind and deaf and the working class; *Rebecca Lukens,* who upon inheriting an iron works mill from her father in the 19th century molded it into a national industry that survives today; *Harriet Martineau,* first woman sociologist (1802—76); *Elizabeth Cady Stanton,* one of the earliest women lawyers and founder of the suffragist movement; *Anne Dudley Bradstreet,* America's first woman poet; *Emma Willard* (1787—1870), first American woman to publicly support higher education for women, and *Frances Willard,* founder of a world temperance union in 1883.

Of more recent vintage are: *Jane Addams,* founder of Hull House in Chicago and the first American woman to win the Nobel Peace prize; *Mrs. Eugenie Anderson,* America's first woman ambassador; *Florence Kelley,* first factory inspector of Illinois; *Sister Elizabeth Kenny,* Australian nurse who originated a special method for treating polio; *Claire Booth Luce,* first U.S. woman ambassador to a major country; *Golda Meir,* prime minister of Israel; *Grandma Moses,* painter who began her career at age 76; *Frances Perkins,* first U.S. woman to hold a cabinet post, and *Nellie Ross,* first governor of a state (Wyoming).

When *Life* magazine prepared a special report on "Remarkable American Women," it began with a list of over 1,000—so obviously the above names are but a few who deserve mention. Apparently it has been easier for women to win fame as authors than in any other profession. Think, for instance, of Louisa May Alcott, Charlotte and Emily Bronte, Pearl Buck, Willa Cather, Agatha Christie, George Eliot (pen name for Mary Ann Evans), Kate Wiggin, Laura Wilder, and dozens of others. Perhaps this entire listing simply gives proof to the statement that "Where there's a will, there's a way"—and as the years go on, for women the way becomes easier.

* * *

Post Script: In 1932, Sigmund Freud, the father of psychoanalysis and one of history's foremost male chauvinists, claimed that women lack strength and independence and are limited by an "original sexual inferiority." But in a recently discovered letter, written in 1938 shortly before he died from cancer, Freud praised his daughter Anna and said that in the face of adversity "in general, women hold up better . . . than do men."

7

Meanwhile, in the church

Rather should the words of the Torah be burned than entrusted to a woman. . . . Whoever teaches his daughter the Torah is like one who teaches her lasciviousness.

Eliezer, a first-century rabbi,
explaining that women may not
study the Scriptures.

Praised be God that He has not created me a gentile . . . a woman . . . or a slave.

Jewish Prayer

When a boy comes into the world, peace comes into the world; when a girl comes, nothing comes.

Even the most virtuous of women is a witch.

Our teachers have said: Four qualities are evident in women: They are greedy at their food, eager to gossip, lazy and jealous.

From the sayings of Palestinian rabbis

You are the devil's gateway . . . you are the first deserter of the divine law; you are she who persuaded him whom the devil was not valiant enough to attack. You destroyed so easily God's image, man. On account of your desert—that is, death—even the Son of God had to die.

Tertullian (160—230)

WHAT IS THE ROLE of women? If the secular world had trouble with this question, the Christian church was no exception, and the answer of some individuals in the church was often far less than what the Bible offered women.

Old Testament women did take part in worship and were required to know the Law. In Deut. 31:12 Moses commands the leaders of Israel to "call together all the men, women, and children" to hear the reading of the Law, and in Joshua 8:34 Joshua reads the whole Law to the entire gathering. Miriam led the women in public rejoicings at the Red Sea. As the women followed her, playing tambourines and dancing, she sang praise "to the Lord, because He has won a glorious victory; He has thrown the horses and their riders into the sea" (Ex. 15:21). Women "served at . . . the tent of the Lord's presence" (Ex. 38:8 and 1 Sam. 2:22), and there were female musicians in the priestly tribes (Neh. 7:67 and Ezra 2:65).

Women held the public office of inspired prophetess, and Deborah served as a judge over God's people.

Nevertheless, in the synagogs the women were separated from the men, a custom which continues to this day among ultra-orthodox Jews, and they were restricted to the women's court, five steps below the men's court. Since all religious life was regulated by the men, the women could not read aloud or take any leadership role.

Another degradation of women was polygamy. The first man in Scripture to have two wives was Lamech, a fifth-generation descendent of Cain. Even at the time of Jesus, polygamy was still legal—for men but not for women. Divorce also was simple for men—they only had to give the woman a writ of divorce, but no Palestinian woman could divorce her husband.

Yet these inquiries amounted to nothing when compared with the ultimate value of the Hebrew faith to women. That value was that men and women worshiped the one true God. Women were not subject to a multitude of lesser goddesses, but they with men were to worship one God—a fact which provides the real foundation for feminine equality. One faith, one Judgment, one Lord, who does not discriminate on the basis of sex.

What a contrast this provided to surrounding peoples and nations! Here is a faith which forbids incest, prostitution, adultery, and license. Here is a faith where all the people are the bride of the Lord and required to be faithful to that God alone. Here is a faith which sees beauty in sex as it relates to marriage (Song of Solomon) and tells the husband to "rejoice with the wife of thy youth."

Yet, lured by the temptations and pagan gods of their neighbors, the Lord's people found it a difficult religion to live, as the plottings of Lot's daughters and the indiscretions of Solomon prove. Priests and prophets repeatedly had to sound dire warnings against sinful pursuits. Over and over they emphasized the many prohibitions found in the Old Testament—and not without cause.

With the coming of Christ, worship practices changed, at least among Christians, to more fully accommodate the concept that before the Lord there is "neither male nor female." The apostles "gathered frequently to pray as a group, together with the women and with Mary the mother of Jesus and with his brothers," according to Acts 1:14. The New Testament church in the house brought men and women together as a worshiping unit not relegated as they had been in the temple to a lower court of women and Gentiles. Although women were not to be "in charge" (1 Cor. 14:34), they could pray and proclaim God's message in public worship (1 Cor. 11:5) so long as they covered their heads. (An uncovered head meant the person was a prostitute. Also the veil was supposed to reduce the temptation caused by women's physical beauty.)

In the ensuing centuries, that beauty came to be seen as a peril to all men, and sexual relationships of any kind were deplored. The highest calling was thought to be celibacy. Many men became monks. St. Jerome, while approving of women as spiritual companions (among his closest friends were Paula and her daughter Eustochium), exhibited a distaste for them as sexual objects. He considered a pregnant woman "a revolting sight" and could not understand why anyone would want to have a child, "a brat . . . to crawl upon his breast and soil his neck with nastiness."

With the fall of the Roman Empire and the conquest by the nominally Christian Germanic tribes, women's role further deteriorated in church and society. Marriage became not a relationship of love, but an important political and commercial transaction in the feudal world. Women "knew well enough that they were not mistresses of their situation, that men regarded them as loot or merchandise, as objects openly and secretly traded among themselves, as prizes sometimes taken by stealth. Lands, men, and crowns might flow from such golden boody."[23]

For some women, convents provided the answer.

> No institution of Europe has ever won for the lady the freedom and development that she enjoyed in the convent in the early days. . . . The lady-abbess was part of the two great social forces of her time, feudalism and the church. She was treated as an equal by the men of her time. . . . She had the stimulus of competition with men in executive capacity, in scholarship, and in artistic production.[24]

Because abbesses often were the pope's or king's representatives in their area, they

> could take their place in political assemblies, such as the Imperial Diet in Germany. They ruled over large domains, held their own judicial courts, and raised armies for their kings as equals with lordly landowners. They were educated to the height of their abilities within the limits of contemporary education.
>
> Beause the monasteries were nearly the only places of education and scholarship throughout most of the Middle Ages and were the repositories of all classical and patristic literature, intellectually inclined women could find satisfaction only in such an environment.[25]

By the 1300s, however, the monastic system had begun to decay. Scholarship decreased, vows of poverty, chastity, and obedience were neglected,

> and persons using the monasteries as an escape from the world far outnumbered those who entered to follow a vocation. Many parents put their young daughters into nunneries for life in order to avoid having to provide (often crippling) dowries. . . .

> Although many of the nuns whose convents were dissolved at the Reformation married (usually former monks), others were totally disoriented after years of sheltered existence, and much hardship ensued. Finally the dissolution of nunneries left a marked gap for women in Protestant countries, which lasted until the nineteenth and twentieth centuries. Not only had nunneries provided a refuge for girls who had little to offer prospective husbands but they had also provided an outlet for women whose talents and interests were not primarily those of wives and mothers and a congenial atmosphere for many widows who ended their years within a nunnery's spiritually and physically comforting walls.[26]

Outside the convent in the Dark Ages, the church at large continued its degeneration of women. Men debated whether women had a soul, and the question found its way to the agenda of the Council at Macon (585), attended by 59 bishops. By a majority of just one vote, they did answer in the affirmative.

By decree of the Council of Auxerre (578), women were forbidden to receive the bread of the Sacrament in their naked hand—they were too impure. Canon law also forbade them to partake of the Eucharist when menstruating.

In addition, Auxerre denied women the right to sing in church, causing church choirs to rely on male eunuchs to sing in the high-pitched voices.

> One of the charges against the Huguenots was that they permitted the women to sing in church, using their voices in praise of God contrary to the express command of St. Paul. . . . The *History of Music* says that when part-singing was first introduced into the

United States, great objection was made to the taking of the soprano or leading part by women, which, by virtue of his superiority, it was declared, belonged to man. Therefore woman was relegated to the bass or tenor. But nature proved too powerful, and man was eventually compelled to take bass or tenor as his part, while women carried the soprano.[27]

When organs were introduced in church worship, women were not allowed to play them because the organ led the singing—and women were not permitted to lead. (A secondary reason for having men organists was the amount of strength required to operate those early organs.)

By the late Middle Ages, for woman it was either the pit or the pedestal. On the one hand, she was the descendant of Eve, the evil temptress, the instrument of the devil; on the other, she was the personification of Mary, the adored Virgin. In support of the latter, a manuscript in the University of Cambridge says,

> Woman is to be preferred to man, to wit: in material, because Adam was made from clay and Eve from the side of Adam; in place because Adam was made outside paradise and Eve within; in conception, because a woman conceived God, which a man could not do; in apparition, because Christ appeared to a woman after the Resurrection, to wit, the Magdalen; in exaltation, because a woman is exalted above the choirs of angels, to wit, the Blessed Mary.[28]

Coupled with the romanticism of chivalry, this view led to the cult of the Virgin. Great cathedrals were built in her honor, pilgrimages were made to her shrines, and her miracles made her the mediatrix between God and man. As the loving mother, portrayed as sorry her children had strayed, Mary provided the warmth needed in a Catholic faith which presented God as prosecutor and Christ as a stern judge.

Protestantism also had a two-edged effect on women. Luther and his followers were the first to recommend public elementary schooling for girls so they could interpret the Bible for themselves and, as mothers, teach their children.[29] Some men later lamented that this placed Bibles in hands that would have been better occupied with a distaff!

> Throughout the centuries following the Reformation the overall literacy rate of Protestant women compared with that of women in Catholic communities (outside of nunneries) was high. In the nineteenth century these literate women of Protestant countries were the backbone of the movements that aimed to give women opportunities for higher education, to enter professions, to administer their own earnings, and to vote.[30]

The other side of the coin was that while Luther supported the priesthood of all believers (men and women), with no priests needed as intermediaries between God and humans, yet the Reformers almost totally reverted to the view of women as taught in the centuries following the early New Testament era. This meant total obedience to husbands, total silence in public, and total preoccupation with the home. The family became an essential unit of government, with the head of the household responsible for seeing that family members were catechized and attended worship services.

And the husband must be obeyed! As William

Gouge explained, "Though an husband in regard of evil qualities may carry the image of the devil, yet in regard of his place and office, he beareth the image of God."[31]

What Luther contributed, though, was a positive view of marriage. He saw woman's ability to bear children as a happy and fortunate destiny and not as the curse defined by earlier churchmen. He saw the sexual side of marriage as a way of expressing mutual love and not solely as an avenue of procreation or a way of avoiding fornication. For Luther, the family and not the convent offered the best of life.

Two unexpected effects of the Reformation were: (1) A nonsacramental view of marriage which necessitated providing other reasons for lifelong commitment within a holy estate; and (2) The appearance of numerous small independent sects. Although deaconesses were ordained by the Eastern Orthodox church in the third century to annoint and prepare women for Baptism, to visit the sick, and to tend the women's entrance to the church, it was the small post-Reformation sects that for the first time permitted women preachers. It is believed the Holland Baptists began the practice, which found its way to Massachusetts by 1636.

But it remained for the Quakers to most completely lift restrictions on women. "All the Friends were allowed to speak and prophesy on a basis of complete equality, for the Inner Light knew no barriers of sex."[32] In most other sects female preaching found its support in the Word of God through Joel, "Afterward I will pour out My Spirit on everyone: your sons and daughters will proclaim My message" (2:28 TEV).

With the coming of the Industrial Revolution,

women were split into two other pit and pedestal categories: the white-gloved upper class lady of society and the working woman (whether in factory or farm or as a houseservant). For those who wanted to serve the church, the deaconess movement was revived.

Its rebirth began in 1836 at Pastor Theodore Fliedner's hospital at Kaisersworth, Germany. His "Institution of Protestant Deaconesses" contained a motherhouse and hospital, a prisoner rehabilitation center, a teacher training school, kindergarten, orphan home, girls' school, a female insane asylum, a women's nursing home, and a deaconess training center. It was here that Florence Nightingale came for nurse's training. Moved by the austere life and the religious dedication of the staff members, who saw themselves as servants of the Lord, she wrote: "Now I know what it is to live and to live life. . . . I wish for no other earth, no other world than this." Her dedication led to fame as superintendent of volunteer nurses during the Crimean War.

Recalling her early desire to serve the church, she wrote to a friend,

> I would have given her (the church) my head, my hand, my heart. She would not have them. She did not know what to do with them. She told me to go back and do crochet in my mother's drawing-room. "You may go to Sunday school if you like," she said. But she gave me no training even for that. She gave me neither work to do for her, nor education for it.[33]

While the church may have done little for the education of women and little to provide service opportunities in the religious sphere, there are many

Christian women who stand out in the pages of history. Lisa Sergio has compiled prayers written by 225 of them in her book, *Prayers of Women.*[34] Edith Deen, in *Great Women of the Christian Faith,*[35] tells the stories of over 120 who stood up for their Lord and shared their faith. More are recorded in religious encyclopedias—and some can even be found in standard encyclopedias.

Although the early women of the church, even the martyrs, are rarely remembered in Protestant circles, they are well known in Roman Catholicism, which has elevated many to sainthood.

How young and dedicated some of the female martyrs were! *Agnes,* for instance, was only 13 when she refused to sacrifice to pagan gods and refused to marry an important Roman who ordered her to renounce her faith. "According to tradition, when she was cast into a burning furnace by his order, a dew descended upon her, miraculously saving her from the flames. Blind with rage, her suitor commanded that she be beheaded."[36]

The first of these women martyrs were *Vibia Perpetua,* a 22-year-old nursing mother, and her slave *Felicity.* The two, along with three male Christians and their teacher, were arrested during a persecution at the beginning of the third century A.D. It was thought that Felicity would not be killed with them because she was pregnant, and it was "illegal to execute a pregnant woman, but three days before the spectacle, Felicity gave birth prematurely to a girl."[37]

The group was flogged, then led to the amphitheater to face wild beasts. Mrs. Deen tells how the men were "attacked by a leopard, a bear and a wild boar," and then the women by "a savage steer."

"Enough!" cried the crowd, after the first attack on the women, so beheading was decreed for them. But "the gladiator was unskilled," Mrs. Dean continues, and on his first attempt, Perpetua received "only slight wounds. After a cry of pain, she herself directed the gladiator's sword to her throat and died."[38]

Her experiences leading to her death were recorded by Perpetua in a book which the New Catholic Encyclopedia calls "one of the most ancient reliable histories of martyrs."[39] The tombs of the two women were discovered in Carthage in 1907, and a basilica has been erected over the spot.

Among the six Catherines who have been canonized by the Catholic Church are:

—*Catherine of Alexandria,* an intelligent and courageous woman who rebuked the emperor for persecuting Christians. He called in some learned philosophers to debate with her, and some of them were converted. Angered, the emperor threw her in prison. When the empress visited her there, the empress was converted—so Catherine was sentenced to die, racked on a spiked wheel. When the wheel broke as they placed her on it, beheading was the verdict.

—*Catherine of Siena* (1348—1380). "No woman in history understood church matters better than the 14th century saint, Catherine of Siena, who was born at a time of nearly unequaled church corruption," writes Mrs. Deen. "She influenced kings and queens and popes alike . . . in carrying out what she felt was the will of God."[40] She selflessly served the sick and dying during the Black Plague but is best remembered for persuading the Papacy to return from France to

Rome, thus bringing a degree of peace to the warring papal states in Italy.

—*Catherine of Genoa* (1447—1510). Married at 16 to a pleasure-loving man, she was converted 10 years later. She then "gave all her time and substance to alleviate the poor. She established hospitals and redressed injustices with such fervor that her husband finally followed her example."[41]

—*Helena* (225—330), mother of Emperor Constantine, also was canonized. "In 326, at great age, she made a visit to the Holy Land, where she founded basilicas on the Mount of Olives and at Bethlehem, (according to later tradition) discovered the cross on which Christ was crucified."[42]

"A community for those wholly devoted to the Christian life" was founded by *Macrina* (327—379) "in the land of Pontus, a strong Christian center and one of the areas to which the First Letter of Peter is written," Mrs. Deen notes. "Here Macrina taught other women the Scriptures in which she was so well versed. Here she established a hospital described as so large that it was 'like a walled city or the pyramids in size.' "[43]

Paula (347—404) was a rich widow who eventually "settled in Bethlehem, where she used her wealth to construct a convent for nuns, a monastery for monks and a guest house for pilgrims. There she devoted her life to works of charity and penance and to the study of the Scriptures, which Jerome says she knew by heart."[44] She assisted Jerome in his Latin translation of the Old Testament, which became the Vulgate (official translation) of the Catholic Church.

Elizabeth of Hungary (1207—1231) is fittingly termed a

"helper of the poor" by Mrs. Deen. "She built a hospital and cared for the sick" and "during a famine she fed nine hundred at her palace gate."[45]

Vittoria Colonna (1490—1547) was a friend of Michelangelo who "inspired this great artist with an ideal of womanhood." She "had the power of making goodness attractive and religion interesting."[46] Would that we could say that of more women today!

With the beginning of the Reformatin, more women stepped forward to offer their talents to the Lord's cause.

Margaret of Navarre (1492—1549), according to Mrs. Deen, "gave refuge to French Reformers in her palace and became a godmother of the Reformation." Her daughter Jeanne "held services for the reformed in her palace apartment and had the Bible translated in the Bernois dialect."[47]

Anne Hutchinson (1591—1643), America's first woman preacher, became one of the founders of Rhode Island when she was "driven out of Massachusetts because of her religious beliefs and teachings, and . . . started her settlement in order to worship as she and her followers liked."[48] Today the First Church of Boston, which tried and banished her in 1637, bears a plaque honoring her as a woman "of ready wit and bold spirit . . . a persuasive advocate of the right of Independent Judgment."

Mary Fisher (1623?—1698?), a Quaker missionary in New England and Turkey, was imprisoned for 16 months "on the charge of 'speaking to a priest'—her own parish minister."[49]

Ann Lee (1736—1784), better known as "Mother Ann," led eight Shakers to America in 1774, making her the first woman to found a religious sect in this country. Although their "shaking, whirling, shouting, prophesying, dancing and singing in strange tongues led to arrests and imprisonment for disturbing the peace," Collier's Encyclopedia says the Shakers were in many respects "the most successful experiment in religious communitarian living in the New World."[50]

Elizabeth Fry (1780—1845), the noted Quaker speaker, campaigned in England and later in Europe for prison reform "which aimed at separation of the sexes, classification of criminals, female supervision of women, and adequate provision of secular and religious instruction. . . . Behind all her philanthropic work, there was a strong Christian impulse and she never ceased to combine it with active evangelization."[51] Mrs. Deen believes Mrs. Fry "accomplished greater prison reforms than any other woman in history."[52]

Ellen White (1827—1915) was considered an "inspired prophetess" by the Seventh day Adventists, who "base their central doctrine on her visions and revelations."[53]

Catherine Booth (1829—1890), wife of the founder of the Salvation Army, "threw herself into evangelization of the masses" after her marriage. "Convinced of the right of women to preach the Gospel, she wrote 'Female Ministry' in 1859. . . . She acquired a great reputation as an orator, holding religious services in London's West End that were attended by people from the highest levels of society."[54]

Nettie Fowler McCormick (1845—1923) "has been called the 'Mother' of the McCormick Theological Seminary in Chicago, to which her family gave more than four million dollars." When she inherited the large estate of her husband, Cyrus, inventor of the grain reaper, she regarded her fortune."as a sacred trust to be used for good causes."[55]

Lottie Moon (1840—1912), founder of the Lottie Moon Christmas offering, has provided, according to Mrs. Deen, more than $50 million to build mission churches, hospitals and homes for missionaries. A native of Virginia, this Southern Baptist spent her life helping the women of China. When famine struck there in 1911, she gave away her rations, eating less and less herself and finally dying of starvation.[56]

Mary Slessor (1848—1915), a redheaded Scottish factory worker, volunteered for Presbyterian mission work at age 27. She was sent to the Calabar Coast of West Africa. Not only did she build churches and schools and help bring law and order, but she was instrumental in ending many tribal abuses, such as murder of twin babies, human sacrifice and witchcraft. "In 1905 the government, recognizing her authority, invested 'Ma Slessor' (as she was popularly called) with the powers of a magistrate, which she continued to exercise until her death."[57]

To this list, Lutherans would add:

—*Katherine von Bora Luther* (1499—1552), whom Martin Luther called his "bright and morning star." As his wife, the former nun managed their home, which had 40 rooms on the first floor alone. She also was "a marvelous hostess—she entertained as many as 120 at a time; and best of all, she succeeded in managing her husband—something a succession of popes were unable to do," comments Charles Ludwig. In his article, "Queen of the Reformation," he says, "Katie Luther was as necessary to the Reformation as the newly invented printing press." Luther said, "I would not exchange Katie for France or Venice. God has given her to me."[58]

—*Rose Young,* educator of Negro children. Concerned about the vast number of uneducated black children living under state laws which made it a crime to teach blacks to read and write, she persevered in seeking church assistance. Through her efforts, Alabama Lutheran Academy and College was established at Selma to train black missionaries and teachers.

—*Gertrude Simon and Olive Gruen,* Lutheran missionaries, remembered for their long selfless service on behalf of the Chinese people from the 1920s to the 1960s. Together they were working at an orphanage when the Japanese invasion forced them to transport 22 children more than 200 miles to safety. The journey took weeks on foot as the two carried their charges, many of them infants, across a mountain range and a major river. Frequently they camped in caves to escape Japanese bombing. After they were forced from China by Communist policies, they continued to work among Chinese refugees—Miss Gruen in Taiwan and Miss Simon in Hong Kong.

—*Deaconess Martha Boss,* Lutheran nurse, teacher, and evangelist, who was a missionary to China and Hong Kong from the 1940s to 1973. She invested her life savings in the Lutheran Handicraft Center so refugees might have a means of livelihood.

—*Dorothy Marple,* assistant to the president of the Lutheran Church in America (LCA) and former executive director of Lutheran Church Women. She also has been dean of women at Thiel College and served as coordinator of the Commission on Function and Structure of the LCA. This Commission drew up the organizational structure under which the LCA now operates.

—*Dr. Dorothy E. L. Haas,* a former director of the Women of the Church in The American Lutheran Church, who later headed the "Women's Desk" of the American Bible Society and did much to encourage women of the U.S. to read the Bible and distribute Scriptures.

8

You've Come a Long Way, Ladies!

Historically the Pauline texts had a backlash effect on our early church fathers. They over-reacted in their interpretation of these to the point where they were reluctant to sanction women's activities of any sort, and were apprehensive over the Biblical 'two or three gathered together in my name' if they happened to be women.

Lu Greenwood in a 1970 presentation
to the LCMS Commission on Mission
and Ministry in the Church

And as for women's organizations, the whole tenor of Scripture indicates that they are not to take the public initiative or leadership in the work of the congregation or the church at large. The limitations of their public activity are too plainly stated to permit of exceptions. Nor may we overlook another factor, namely, that large organizations or federations of women's clubs within the church are in danger of becoming busybodies in other men's matters, since their enthusiasm for the cause in which they believe is apt to lead them to a propaganda that may interfere with the work of the individual congregation.

P. E. Kretzmann (1930)
in Concordia Theological Monthly

> Ever since Jesus Christ came to this earth, the status of women in the world has been rising. They are regarded by the heathen as slaves or mere property. But in the priesthood of all believers and before God they are placed on an equality with men. St. Paul says: "There is neither male nor female; for you are all one in Christ Jesus" (Gal. 3:28). Women's status has been rising in society, in business, in education, and at long last in the church. The former practice of keeping woman in her place in the home is turning into giving woman her proper place in the church as a respected and capable servant of God who does not try to usurp authority over the man. Jesus not only raised the status of women but has given her a responsibility too. As He Himself was "about His Father's business," so He expects women to be about their Father's business.
>
> Rev. Elmer Kettner in
> "Women's Work in the Church,"
> a Concordia Tract Mission tract

YES, THE STATUS of women is rising. Ladies have come a long way—and particularly in the church during the last century. A news release issued in 1977 by the Lutheran Council in the USA gives a hint at changing attitudes.

It describes a church in North Carolina which, in response to a Lutheran World Relief appeal for blankets, set up a "blanket factory," with the men challenged to help.

> The first Wednesday evening in June a dozen men showed up. Waiting for them were 80 pounds of "ends" purchased from a blanket manufacturer, a couple of heavy duty sewing machines alongside several home portables, and two local tailors.

For an hour and a half the men got a quick course in sewing. The conversations went something like this:

"This is a bobbin."

"What's a bobbin?"

"You put it in the bobbin case. Drop it in and put the needle down like this. . . . This pedal is like driving a car—you just give it some gas."

"That's my speed!"

"This is a seam."

"That's the first thing you've said that I could understand."

The "varsity sewers" then went to work. Their output—eight blankets.

The next week the "factory" rolled again, with the women involved. More heads devised a better system, and more hands used up all the material. Their total output—33 blankets.

"We had a good time doing it," reported the pastor who coordinated the project. Along with an "old-fashioned satisfaction of using one's own hands to supply another's need" came "the renewed awareness about unknown people around the world whose plight makes an available blanket good news."

That story represents two important attitude changes: today's men are not ashamed to do traditional women's work, and today's men are willing and able to demonstrate publicly that they care about people. No longer do emotion, tears, and loving concern have totally feminine connotations.

So recent are such changes in the church, though, that most parishes have people who can remember:

—When men used to sit on one side of the church and women and children on the other for Sunday worship (they still do in some Jewish synagogs).

—When hiring a woman parochial school teacher was appropriate only as an emergency solution during a shortage of men teachers.

—When first attempts to found church women's organizations were repressed by the men.

—When women were not permitted to vote at congregational meetings.

—When female teachers were paid lower wages than men for the same work.

—When the first Deaconess Training School was opened by the Lutheran Synodical Conference.

—When church colleges were not coeducational.

—When women's role was defined by the German proverb—"Kinder, Kirche, und Kueche" (children, church and kitchen).

—When the first women were appointed to District and synodical committees and commissions of the church.

While the Saxons who were to found The Lutheran Church—Missouri Synod were sailing to America, they began on shipboard to make plans for the education of their children. Although there had been no women teachers in Germany, it was only a few years after they set foot on this continent that they began to allow women to teach.

This posed another problem—proper training. The first proposal for a seminary for women was made in 1873, but few students applied and the idea was dropped. Another 46 years elapsed before any women were trained in the Misouri Synod college system. In 1919 five women entered Concordia Teachers College, Seward, Nebr.

It took seven more years, however, for the Synod to

put its official stamp of approval on this action. In a 1926 resolution, the synodical convention, noting that such training of women was "carried on without particular expense to Synod," decreed that enrollment of "female pupils" should not exceed 20 percent of the total enrollment at Seward. That same convention also approved admission of women to the college at Edmonton, Alberta, Canada, with the same 20 percent restriction.

In the 50 years leading up to this resolution, there was considerable debate about the appropriateness of women as teachers, perhaps accounting for the many delayed decisions in the face of mounting concern about training for women teachers. An article in 1897 concluded that it is "proper to employ women as teachers because the church can institute new offices, which are helper offices to the pastor. These offices are to be filled according to the gifts God gives His people. Teaching is one of these offices, and many young women and widows have the gift to teach children, especially young children. Thus it is proper and even essential for the church to use these gifts in filling the office of teacher of children."[59]

However an article in a 1925 *Lutheran School Journal* complained that there were not enough men teachers, especially in the public schools. The author felt the large number of women teachers was dangerous "because the feminine example of a woman teacher would hinder the development of manly qualities in boys. He also claimed that girls needed this manly example of male teachers to more fully develop their feminine qualities."[60]

In response to a further objection to women

teachers, the Synod's 1929 convention stated that "the calling of men must remain the rule and order in the Synod. However if there are not enough men, it may be necessary to call a woman teacher temporarily until she can be replaced by a man." Men are always to be preferred, even in the lower grades, the convention noted, adding that there would always be some women teachers. Churches that employ women were advised to be sure they have good training. Despite this admonishment, the convention refused to allow coeducation at Concordia College, Oakland, Calif. By 1930 there were 500 women teachers, only 10 percent of them trained in Synodical schools.[61]

The prevailing opinion seemed to be: soon we will have enough men trained and will not need the women; therefore we won't open any more training opportunities for females. And that nearly came to pass during the depression. As the number of teaching positions dwindled, there were almost enough men.

With money scarce, one experienced woman teacher was fired so that a male graduate could be hired at a reduced rate. When she complained, she was told by a church official that women teachers had always been considered temporary to fill an emergency situation, and now that there were enough men, "she should willingly step down and be thankful she had had the opportunity to serve."[62]

The emergency was short-lived. After the depression, the number of women teachers climbed, and by 1959 there were 3,000, compared with only 2,000 men, teaching in parochial schools. Eventually women were admitted for training at every synodical educational institution, even the seminaries (although women may not be ordained).

Acceptance of this teaching role for women was acknowledged in a variety of studies and resolutions:

—A 1941 study on the status of women teachers stated that as a religious instructor, she carries out the function of the ministry, and her position in the classroom is no different than the male teacher, although she is subordinate to men in general and a servant of the congregation.

—A 1965 convention report said that properly certified teachers have a call, and their induction into office should be a "commissioning" or a "consecration." They are to be considered "installed" and are to follow the same procedures as men teachers when transferring from one school to another.

—Women are to be given equal pay for equal work, according to a 1973 convention resolution. Moreover, women now serve on faculties of Synod's institutions of higher education.

If it was difficult for girls who wanted to be teachers to find a college in which to study, it was even more so for girls who wanted a general education in a coeducational religious setting. "Women are inferior and need protection," said early opponents of coeducation, explaining,

> At home and in society the girls can choose their own associates with the proper aid of the parents. In a school they cannot do this. The daughter of refined parents may be alphabetically placed next to a boy with the manners of a slouch, and in this way become injuriously affected.[63]

Fears of flirtations, scandal, and early engagements

and marriages were voiced. Supporters of coeducation suggested that girls would give the fellows stiffer competition and make them more gentlemanly. Retorted an opponent: "I have never heard of anybody doing great things resulting from competition with girls in school. . . . coeducation has the disadvantage of lessening man's instinctive respect for womanhood."

At Luther College, Decorah, Iowa, the problem was solved in 1932 by "sneaking them in the back door." When the Board of Trustees turned down a request for coeducation, in July 1932, Decorah townspeople arranged to open Decorah Junior College for Girls. With the approval of Luther's president, O. J. Preus, the girls were allowed to use the college's science labs and library. The next year they also attended classes and chapel at the college, and finally in 1936, Luther officially admitted women. The only restrictions: the girls had to sit in the last two rows of the chapel and they could not eat in the boys' dining hall.

Deaconesses fared somewhat better. When the first Lutheran hospital in America was started in Pittsburgh in 1849, four deaconesses were brought over from Germany to serve as nurses. Eventually, the United Lutheran Church founded a motherhouse in Philadelphia (1884) and others followed. Finally in 1919 a Lutheran Deaconess Association, with headquarters in Fort Wayne, was organized by Associated Lutheran Charities for women of the Synodical Conference. Prime mover in the effort was Rev. F. W. Herzberger, who wrote a tract on "Woman's Work in the Church."

To illustrate the need for women's service in the church, he told the story of two farmers. Seeing storm clouds gathering, Farmer A called the women of the

family to assist. He got his crops harvested before the storm. Farmer B tried to do it himself. His crop was lost. Farmer A represented other Protestant churches; Farmer B, the Synodical Conference.
Pastor Herzberger asked:

> Why have we Lutherans of the Synodical Conference failed so far to make use of the many gifted and pious women the Lord has given also to us for work in the fields entrusted to our stewardship? Are we living in a different world from that in which the Christians of other denominations are living—a world less affected by sin and want and woe than theirs? Certainly not. We meet the same wants and afflictions they have to contend with in their church work. As they, so do we need the assistance of trained women workers in our various harvest fields.

Organization of church women's groups began much earlier in most denominations. Their purpose: not self-assertion but missionary support. Led by Mary Webb, Baptist and Congregational women formed The Boston Female Society for Missionary purposes in 1800. Presbyterian women followed suit in 1817, and a Methodist branch began in 1832. The Episcopalians authorized a Women's Auxiliary to the Board of Missions in 1871. All were concerned with overseas mission work, but in 1880 the first home mission group was started by the Methodists to assist with work among Southern blacks. First president of this Women's Home Missionary Society was Mrs. Rutherford B. Hayes, wife of the president of the U.S.

Despite the early start among Baptist women, it was not until 1877 that plans were made to begin a woman's society in every Baptist church. Even then progress was slow—some pastors sat in stony silence when asked to supply names of women who might be interested in organizing. In Kentucky the names eventually were secured with the cooperation of postmasters.[64]

Other firsts during this period included:

—Introduction of mite boxes as a fund-raising device by the Woman's Mission to Woman (Baptist) in 1871.

—Publication of an 8-page monthly by the Methodist Woman's Home Missions in 1884. Price: 25¢ per year.

—Beginning of seaport hospice work by women in 1884.

In Lutheran circles, women's work took various forms. The first missionary sent out by the United Lutheran Church was educated for his work and supported in the field totally by women who began the Female Association of Hartwick Synod for the Education of Foreign Missionaries. In Milwaukee women organized to build a church. A sewing circle in Decorah began meeting in 1862 to sew and sell articles to help pay the debt on the new Luther College there. That same year a Ladies Aid in St. Ansgar, Iowa, brought two boys to the U.S. from Madagascar and educated one to be a minister and the other a teacher.

Formal organization in 1879 of a churchwide mission society in the United Lutheran Church (now part of the Lutheran Church in America) was motivated by a story about two women who wanted to be missionaries but were refused because the church body lacked funds. What's needed, said a college professor's wife, is "a little systematic and united effort," and she began to provide that.

It was a desire to sew, mend, wash, and iron for ministerial students that led to the first women's groups in the Missouri Synod. Almost simultaneously, ladies organized in Fort Wayne and St. Louis, where the Synod's two seminaries were located. After the women patched a garment, "it often reminded one of Joseph's coat of many colors,"[65] according to a report in a college publication. The St. Louis group, known as Frau Doktor Walther's Naehverein (Mrs. Walther's Sewing Circle), sewed and talked and enjoyed coffee and coffeecake—and grew in faith.

> On one occasion, the society met during an unusually dry period of the year. Much lamentation regarding the drought was heard at this meeting. After having listened for some time to the complaints, Mrs. Walther arose and said: "My dear friends, we don't pray enough; this drought is due partly to the lack of prayer. Let us all kneel and fervently petition the Lord to send us rain." All knelt while Mrs. Walther led in prayer. Thereupon the women busied themselves again with their task of sewing for the needy students, when, lo and behold, from the distance there came sounds of rolling thunder, the sun became obscured, clouds gathered, lightning flashed, and even before the meeting adjourned their prayer was answered as a welcome rain refreshed the parched earth.[66]

Although women began to organize mission support groups in many congregations for the benefit of orphan homes, hospitals, and India and China missions, it was not until 1941 that Missouri Synod women obtained permission to launch a national women's organization. To accomplish this, the women and their pastoral supporters had to overcome the doubts and objections of church leaders. "It would be difficult," said one, "for our District officers to control so many organized women." An elderly pastor warned against the danger of feminism in the church. "Their support of special projects will decrease their contributions to Synod," feared another.

Others reiterated some of the philosophy expressed by Dr. Wilhelm Sihler, president of the Fort Wayne seminary, in an 1872 article on "Woman's Vocation and Its Deterioration."

"In her domestic and material calling, according to God's will and ordinance, the purpose of woman is fulfilled," Dr. Sihler believed.

> The man's calling is different. It is he alone who is to make laws, supervise their enforcement, institute justice and righteousness on earth, and render due obedience to existing laws. He alone according to God-given gifts, is appointed, according to his calling, within the community, either to till the soil or to convert raw materials into manufactured products for the common good, for this purpose even to harness the powers of nature, such as steam, water, light, electricity. It is he alone through whom, according to the special gifts of God, by his calling, the world of the sciences and the fine arts is opened up; yes, also in the community of the church it is the man alone—for "the women are to keep silence in the church"—who is officially to administer God's Word and sacraments publicly.[67]

Against this background, imagine then the excitement when the first area meetings were proposed for women of neighboring societies.

It was in horse-and-buggy times that the women of Zion Lutheran Church, Wausau, received an invitation from the women of a Merrill parish to attend a joint meeting. The opportunity of going away for a day was a treat—but Zion members had never thought of such a thing, reports an article in the *Lutheran Woman's Quarterly*.

> In fact there was still some opposition against homemakers joining Aid societies that met on weekday afternoons. The opposers, men and women, claimed that a Kaffee Klatch, as they preferred to call any Aid meeting, was only a good way to neglect home duties. Thus to take a day off for a meeting—out of town yet—was definitely out of the ordinary.
>
> Moreover, some of the members had not even been to Merrill, although it was less than 20 miles away. Yes, there were livery stables where horses and vehicles could be rented, but most of the city folks did this only on special occasions like funerals or weddings.
>
> To get to the meeting at Merrill meant a round trip on the Chicago, Milwaukee, & St. Paul R.R., leaving Wausau between 8 and 9 in the morning and returning just before 8 o'clock in the evening.
>
> The chosen date was a beautiful early June day. White trilliums were scattered in clumps among the grass, and here and there vistas of the Wisconsin River could be seen from the train.
>
> Thrilling to the unknown ahead, each woman took good care of the paper bearing the name of her own hostess for the day. Because only a few had relatives in Merrill, most of the ladies had been assigned to hostesses whom they had never met.

When the train arrived, the guests were welcomed by the president of the Merrill Ladies Aid. Businessmen and a few others who owned cars took the women to the homes of their hostesses. For some, this was their first ride in an automobile!

At the homes, they met their hosts and had noon dinner. . . . After dinner, all were taken to church in time for the meeting. A worthwhile, interesting program had been arranged. Guest speakers pointed out the fellowship benefits of larger get-togethers.

At the brief business meeting, a motion was made and carried that proceeds of the freewill offering be given to a mission project, and a precedent was established.

One of the last numbers on the program had to be omitted to allow enough time for lunch before the train was due. Back home again, no ill effects due to Mama's 12-hour absence were found. (In those days everybody said "papa" and "mama." To say "father" or "mother" was considered "oldish and Dutchy."

Next year another "annual meeting" was held. By 1926 dinners in homes were discontinued in favor of a meal served at the meeting site.

At first all the conventions were conducted in German. There were no mimeographed programs and topic sheets, but speakers did choose educational subjects related to Christian living.

During a convention held in a presidential election year, the women were reminded to exercise their right to vote. Many ladies felt they were not yet well enough versed in politics and would have to ask, "Papa, fuer wen soll ich stimmen?" (Papa, for whom am I to vote?)

At the 1930 convention, mothers were advised to

> discipline their children when the need arose and not put it off with, "Wart, bis Papa heimkommt" (Wait till papa comes home). The speaker pointed out that papa, being gone all day, was not in a position to judge the situation as well as mama, who had been on the spot when the crime called for swift and certain punishment. . . .
>
> As time went on, the steady growth of the conventions brought the need for forenoon and afternoon sessions. The change in language developed gradually with English and German numbers on the programs at first—and then entirely English.[68]

Now, over 50 years later, the Lutheran Women's Missionary League is an international organization of the Missouri Synod (200,000 members who raise $1 million a year for district and international projects). Women have the vote in over 60 percent of the parishes. They teach Sunday school and vacation Bible school. They lead prayers and Bible studies. They usher and read the Gospel and Epistle in some parishes, and on LWML Sunday they often help plan the service. They serve on commissions of the Synod, and they are called as Directors of Christian Education in parishes which do not have a parochial school.

Great progress, yes, but in the world, other changes were taking place. . .

9

A Long Way— But Far Enough?

In the male-dominated Victorian culture, women "are declared to be better than men; an empty compliment which must provoke a bitter smile from every woman of spirit, since there is no other situation in life in which it is the established order, and considered quite natural and suitable, that the better should obey the worse."

John Stuart Mill,
in his 1869 essay
on "The Subjection of Women"

The moment they begin to be your equals, they will be your superiors.

Cato (195 B.C.)

Nature gave women too much power; the law gives them too little.

Will Henry

Women have been dehumanized—more than anyone else. But a counter-revolution is beginning a return to reality.

Dr. J. A. O. Preus, as quoted
in July 1971 "Adam's Rib"

Woman's place is in the House—and in the Senate!
decal on a tee shirt Decal on a tee shirt

Cartoon showing young girl watching mother prepare supper: "You're a good cook, Mom. I hope my husband is as good a cook as you."

Discrimination against women is incompatible with human dignity and with the welfare of the family and of society, prevents their participation, on equal terms with men, in the political, social, economic and cultural life of their countries and is an obstacle to the full development of the potentialities of women in the service of their countries and of humanity. . . .

The full and complete development of a country, the welfare of the world and the cause of peace require the maximum participation of women as well as men in all fields.

From introduction to the "Declaration on the Elimination of Discrimination Against Women," adopted by the United Nations General Assembly
Nov. 7, 1967

YES, women obviously have come a long way—but today's feminists say it's not far enough! As continuing goals, they list equal pay for work of equal value, equal employment and advancement opportunities, equal political representation, equal treatment under the law, equal education, and 24-hour childcare centers for working women.

Their goals draw mixed reactions from women as well as men, possibly because "women's lib" and "Equal Rights Amendment" mean different things to different people.

Some equate "liberation" with protesting women shattering teacups in Rochester, N.Y. . . . or the Syracuse "baby-in" when 50 children were left at city hall to impress the mayor with the need for childcare centers . . . or angry bra-burners who object to cosmetics, deodorants, and wedding gowns.

For some women, the words create fear of compulsory military service, common toilets, and loss of privileges and protection which they value.

Others identify feminism with the International Women's Year Conference in Mexico City in 1975, where despite disagreements, the 1,300 delegates and 7,000 visitors from 130 countries produced a "World Plan of Action."

For some the words mean hope of improved inheritance laws for farm wives (so exhorbitant death taxes will not force them to sell the land they worked so hard to develop with their husbands) . . . and hope of social security coverage for homemakers, more equitable property division in case of divorce, and equality in property ownership and credit laws.

Some men feel threatened by ERA as they envision increased competition for jobs and education—but other men are adding their "amens" to to the words of *Washington Post* writer Nicholas Von Hoffman, who looks forward to the demise of "frilly ninnies" who "use Comet to scour their brain pans clean of every last crumb of thought."

Whatever the reaction to women's liberation, one thing is obvious to anyone who takes a look at history—the movement is not a new one, not even in the United States.

Suffragist Alice Paul has noted that the first petition

for women's suffrage in this hemisphere was presented in 1648 by Margaret Brent, whom encyclopedias identify as the first woman in America to hold business and professional positions previously limited to men.

As patriots were demanding a Declaration of Independence in 1776, Abigail Adams wrote to her president husband, John:

> In the new Code of Laws . . . I desire you would Remember the Ladies, and be more generous and favorable to them than your ancestors. Do not put such unlimited power into the hands of the Husbands. Remember all Men would be tyrants if they could. If particular care and attention is not paid to the Ladies we are determined to foment a Rebellion, and will not hold ourselves bound by any Laws in which we have no voice, or Representation.
>
> That your Sex are Naturally Tyranical is a Truth so thoroughly established as to admit of no dispute, but such of you as wish to be happy willingly give up the harsh title of Master for the more tender and endearing one of Friend. Why then, not put it out of the power of the vicious and the Lawless to use us with cruelty and indignity with impunity. Men of Sense in all Ages abhor those customs which treat us only as the vassals of your Sex. Regard us then as Beings. . . .

Calling his wife "saucy," John responded, "Depend upon it we know better than to repeal our Masculine systems."

No organized effort to secure women's rights developed, however, until the 1800s after the Industrial Revolution opened more and more factory jobs for women. (The one exception—and rather short-lived at that—was in New Jersey, where women were given the right to vote from 1790 to 1807.)

Still bound by the patterns of English common law, American women had few legal rights. Even money or property which they inherited reverted to their husbands. Finally, married women campaigned in New York to revise property laws. Result: an 1848 bill which gave them the right to own real estate in their own name.

That same year 250 women and 40 men came by horse and buggy and wagon to a meeting in Seneca Falls, N.Y. There they issued a Declaration of Sentiment which said, "We hold these truths to be self-evident: that all men and WOMEN are created equal. . . ." They demanded free speech and opportunities for women in business, trade, and education.

The convention was called by Elizabeth Cady Stanton and Lucretia Coffin Mott, who were incensed because they, as women, had been denied seats on the main floor at a world antislavery meeting in London. Women, they concluded, were just as much enslaved by white men as were the blacks.

From then on, national women's rights conventions were held annually until the start of the Civil War. During discussions on inheritance and property rights, suffrage, divorce laws, and guardianship of children, the recurring question was, "Should rights or the vote get first priority?" If women can vote, they will have the power to achieve the rest, it was decided.

Their cause was most unpopular. "Preachers likened them to prostitutes; angry mobs pelted them with everything from prayer books to rotten eggs because of their 'unladylike' behavior," reports June Brady Csida.[69]

All male citizens received the right to vote under the 14th amendment in 1868, and the same privilege was extended to black males in 1870. No such luck for the ladies—although a few states provided exceptions. Wyoming, for instance, granted women equal rights, including suffrage, in 1869. (Wyoming also elected the nation's first woman governor—Mrs. Nellie Taylor Ross in 1924. She later became the first woman director of the U.S. Mint.)

It was not just illegal, but a crime, for women to vote in most states, as Susan B. Anthony and 15 followers proved. In November 1872 they were arrested for going to the polls in Rochester, N.Y., where they did "knowingly, wrongfully, and unlawfully vote for a representative to the Congress of the United States."

Nevertheless, that same year the first woman ran for President. She was Victoria Woodhull, a believer in spiritualism, healing, and free love. This latter interest severly damaged the cause of women's rights, particularly when she ended up in jail on election day. The charge: obscenity. In her newspaper, she had printed the story of preacher Henry Ward Beecher's alleged affair with a married parishioner. (Adding insult to injury was the fact that Beecher was a past president of the American Woman Suffrage Association.)

Beginning in 1878, an amendment to give women full suffrage was introduced in every session of Congress. Not until 1919, when the war demanded the full cooperation of women, was it passed by both houses. Ratification by 36 states made it law in 1920. Other countries were more progressive—New Zealand granted women the right to vote in 1893; Finland, 1906;

Norway, 1907; Australia, 1908; Denmark and Iceland, 1915; Russia, 1917; Canada, Germany, Luxembourg, and Poland, 1918.

Many modern women's organizations which have been supportive of ERA trace their roots to women's concerns of a century ago. The American Association of University Women began in 1882 as a group to study women's health. Their goal was to show that women's health was not damaged by the intellectual strain of schooling.

When the all-male New York Press Club would not admit a newspaperwoman, Mrs. Jane C. Crolly, to a dinner honoring Charles Dickens, she organized the Sorosis Club, which became the General Federation of Women's Clubs.

Former suffrage workers formed the League of Women voters in 1920 to educate women in their electoral responsibilities, and protests seemingly became a thing of the past as women walked through the new doors opening to them. The National Women's Party, organized in 1913 to support the suffrage movement, spearheaded the introduction of the first Equal Rights Amendment to Congress in 1923, but it got nowhere.

Education and employment were the new priorities. Descendants of the crusaders determined to try both. Advanced education degrees were earned in the 1930s by the highest proportion of U.S. women in this country's history—and that percentage has not yet been topped. During World War II, 18 million held jobs in industry, with many war plants and churches providing nurseries for workers' children. Although some female workers returned to homemaking duties after the war, the number employed outside the home has remained high—over 40%.

As they worked, these women became increasingly aware of inequities in pay and advancement. Result: The calm ended—the storm broke loose again.

What actually launched the rebirth of feminism in the 1960s?

Some say it was the Civil Rights protests. When the idealistic young women joined the cause, they saw the men making all the decisions. The only time the gals found themselves in the forefront was when the police were expected.

Others credit Betty Friedan's "The Feminine Mystique," published in 1963, and similar books which followed: "Sexual Politics," by Kate Millet: "The Female Eunuch," by Germaine Greer, and Caroline Bird's "Born Female."

One thing is sure—it did not result from the sexual revolution! The sexual revolution was extremely destructive to women, says Robin Morgan, founder of WITCH (Women's International Terrorist Conspiracy from Hell). "It never helped us—it just made us more available."

Another feminist known as Laura X says that since the advent of the birth control pill, "men have become no more human: according to many young women who have made that unenviable leap from private property to public property, they treat women worse than ever."

"The modern Women's Liberation Movement is as much a state of mind as a visible, organized drive to attain certain social and political goals," says Csida.[70] At its core, lending encouragement to the hundreds of consciousness-raising groups which meet weekly to share concerns, are numerous organizations, including NOW (National Organization of Women). Founded by Friedan in 1966, NOW acts "to bring women into full participation in the mainstream of American Society, *now,* assuming all the privileges and responsibilities thereof in fully equal partnership with men."

Other organizations include Federally Employed Women (FEW), Women, Inc., of San Francisco, Women's Equity Action League (WEAL), National Women's Political Caucus, Media Women, and more radical groups such as BITCH (for nothing), WITCH, Bread and Roses (meaning that women want not only flowers but bread, i.e., wages), Redstockings, the Radical Mothers, SCUM (Society for Cutting Up Men), and the Feminists.

Groups also have sprung up in opposition to ERA—for example, HOW (Happiness of Womanhood), Men Our Masters, Pussycat League, and the followers of Phyllis Schlafly and the "Total Woman" concepts of Marabel Morgan.

Despite such opposition, it's obvious that time, inventions and feminism have combined in the past 20 years to bring changes galore to the lives of women.

Employer demand for women job applicants increased 50% in 1974 over the previous year, according to a national sampling of college placement directors.

"Working Woman" is a new magazine aimed at the 38 million working women in the U.S. (That figure represents an increase of 15 million since 1960.)

The roles of truck driver, wrestler, police, jockey, game warden, race driver, airline pilot, Rhodes scholar, corporation board member, and bank president have lost their "men only" label, to mention just a few. A woman conducts the Opera Company of Boston and has directed the New York Metropolitan Opera. President Nixon appoitned a recruiter of women for government appointments. President Carter named Juanita Kreps Secretary of Commerce. During President Ford's term, Shirley Temple Black, former ambassador to Ghana, became the first woman to serve as chief of protocal.

Of the 52 women who ran for the House of Representatives in 1976, 18 were elected. In 1970 there were only 25 female contenders.

The number of women in state legislatures rose to 9.1% in 1976 (double the number of 1970).

An organization for Executive Women in Government has over 100 members in Washington, D.C.

The Chicago White Sox broadcast team now includes a woman, and women are appearing more regularly as newscasters, weather forecasters, and sportscasters on local TV and radio stations. Barbara Walters moved up to a status previously denied American women when she signed a $5 million contract for five years with ABC television in 1976. To the chagrin of men, she was paid more as a newcomer than her male counterparts received after years of experience.

Management Woman, Inc., is a firm which locates women for executive jobs paying $25,000 or more a year. Their fees are paid by the companies that hire the women.

A women's bank has been organized in New York City "to cater to the special needs of women who have money or who have been denied money; to provide careers in banking for women; and to capitalize on what may be an expanding market."

The House voted in 1976 to disband the Women's Army Corps and its sister military organizations and in the interests of equality to include women in the regular military services. The Navy has named its first woman admiral, and the Army and Air Force, their first women generals.

Women delegates to political conventions have doubled.

Wisconsin law includes Susan B. Anthony's birthday, Feb. 15, among 10 days to be given special observance in state public schools.

A woman is leading a drive to unionize housemaids.

From 1970 to 1975, college enrollment of older women increased 30%.

The 3M Company of St. Paul, Minn., was ordered to pay $111,557 to 10 women who were discriminated against in salary because of their sex "and in some cases were cursed at, laughed at or harassed with pornographic material."

The U.S. Fourth Circuit Court of Appeals in Virginia ruled that a woman who loses her job because she refuses sexual advances of a male boss has a right to sue her former employer for damages under the Civil Rights Act.

The New York City Council has lifted its 115-year-old ban on women venders at such public places as baseball parks and football stadiums.

Girls competitive sports are becoming increasingly popular. Intercollegiate athletic conferences have been organized in many girls sports, and high schools and colleges and increasing their girls athletic program budgets.

The National Rifle Association is actively recruiting female members for its battle against gun control.

Statistics for 1974 showed violent juvenile female crime was 30% higher than 1960. (Obviously, not all the news is positive!)

And, women have qualities that make them better gamblers than men, according to an article in "Gambling Times." The qualities: motivation (they gamble for practical reasons—they know what they want to buy with any winnings) and orderliness (they do a better job of following a plan of betting).

Punitive damages up to $10,000 are permitted in court suits brought by women who have been denied credit on the same terms that men are granted it.

The Lucy Stone League, founded in 1921 to help married women retain their own family name, has its modern counterpart in the Center for a Woman's Own Name, founded in 1973 in Illinois.

Names of wives as well as husbands may be listed in phone books now.

As of Jan. 1, 1977, housewives who do not hold a paying job become eligible for tax-sheltered individual retirement accounts in their own name—a privilege their husbands had previously enjoyed. Homemaker-husbands also will benefit under this ruling.

Yes, men are benefitting too! Men's liberation groups have been formed to give men an opportunity to talk about how the male role oppresses them. Men have been granted paternity leave, so they can spend an equal amount of time with their children. Women in Communications, Inc., now admits men as members. Men are now serving as male day care workers and nursery school teachers.

And in England, a 22-year-old man won a sex discrimination suit, claiming he was refused a job in a pub because he was not a buxom barmaid.

A 1974 poll showed that 50% of American Women favor efforts to strengthen and change their status. The other half is split between those who resist such action (29%) and those who haven't made up their minds or are ignoring the issue (21%).

Compare this with a 1971 Harris poll which found 42% of all women opposed to women's rights action. By 1972, that percentage was reduced to 36%—and the poll also revealed that 42% of the men favored feminist progress.

Much of the progress can be directly traced to recent action of Congress.

Under Section 7.03 of the Civil Rights Act of 1964, employers are prohibited from hiring, firing, or in other ways discriminating against any individual for reasons of race, color, religion, or sex. Ironically, the inclusion of the word "sex" was a maneuver by a Southern congressman who opposed the racial freedoms of the bill. He hoped the sex provision would cause it to fail.

Adding teeth to the bill was the authorization in 1972 for the Equal Employment Opportunity Commission to sue employers in Federal court for not complying with Section 7.

Provisions of the 1963 Equal Pay Act were extended in 1972 to women in professorial, managerial, and administrative positions of universities receiving Federal grants, under Title 9 of the 1969 Higher Education Act. Sex discrimination in admissions policies was prohibited by that 1969 Act, and a review of discriminatory practices at such institutions resulted in lawsuits against 350 schools.

In a 1973 landmark case related to equal rights, American Telephone and Telegraph agreed to pay $15 million in back pay to 15,000 employees and provide goals and timetables for increased utilization of women and racial/ethnic minorities.

In the first known equal pay ruling for public school teachers, the Labor Department in 1977 won back wages for 120 Texas women who were paid less than their male colleagues.

In 1971 the Supreme Court determined that unequal treatment based only on sex violated the 14th amendment, which provides all citizens with equal protection under the law.

Finally in March 1972, almost 50 years after it was first introduced, an Equal Rights Amendment was passed by Congress. The amendment reads: "Equality of rights under the law shall not be denied or abridged by the United States or by any state on account of sex."

If approval of 38 states is not achieved by 1979, the amendment will be lost. As of 1977, only 35 states had ratified it, and future prospects appear slim. "It's dead, it's dead forever," shouted a North Carolina senator after the ERA defeat in his state.

Commenting on the ERA battle, columnist James J. Kilpatrick noted,

> So long as change comes little by little, a society adapts. But the fear is that changes resulting from the ERA might prove to be drastic changes—changes a startled people couldn't get out of. . . . For my own part, I hope the amendment fails, but I hope its purpose succeeds. It may be a fine idea to eliminate

sexual distinctions from every nook and cranny of the law, but a small voice whispers that we might be happier to end them in *almost* every nook and cranny instead.

Whatever the outcome, it will not end the women's rights movement in the U.S. Although the wheels of justice may grind more slowly without a constitutional amendment, proponents of women's equality will continue their struggle through court action, based on the Civil Rights Act and other laws previously cited.

Motivation will come in part from the fact that the effort is not unique to the United States. Leading the way is the United Nations, which has had a Commission on the Status of Women since 1946.

"The universal recognition in law and in fact of the principle of equality of men and women" is the purpose of the UN's Declaration on the Elimination of Discrimination Against Women, passed in 1967. It advocated:

—Abolition of all existing laws, customs, regulations and practices which are discriminatory against women;

—Eradication of prejudice and all other practices which are based on the idea of the inferiority of women;

—Equal rights to vote in all elections and hold public office;

—The same rights as men to acquire, change or retain nationality;

—Equal rights with men under civil law, including property rights, equality of status of husband and wife, free choice of spouse, and equal rights and duties relating to children.

—Equal educational rights at all levels;

—Equal rights in the field of economic and social life, including right to free choice of profession and employment, and professional and vocational advancement without discrimination on grounds of marital status.

The UN Commission also has sponsored seminars in Colombia (1953), Ethiopia (1960), and England (1973), all of which brought women together from all over the world to discuss their common concerns.

Culminating these efforts was the observance of 1975 as International Women's Year. Preparation for U.S. participation began in 1972 when the State Department set up a planning group and eventually established an IWY Secretariat. A 35-member National Commission was created by President Ford.

Under the theme, "Equality, Development, and Peace," a World Conference was held in Mexico City from June 19 to July 2, 1975. Delegates adopted a World Plan of Action for the Implementation of the Objectives of the International Women's Year. Its outline for national action covers the strengthening of international peace, political participation, education and training, employment and economic roles, health and nutrition, the family in modern society, population, housing and related facilities, and social questions. It made proposals in regard to research, data collection and analysis, mass communication, and global and regional action.

The Conference also called for a "Decade for Women" (1975—85), with another conference to be held in 1980 (the midpoint).

As an IWY followup, state meetings were held

across the U.S. in 1977, involving women of all ages, incomes, ethnic, racial, and religious backgrounds. Funded with Federal money, the meetings provided government backing to press for changes in policies that obstruct women's equality. Handbook for all the meetings, as well as the concluding national gathering in Texas, was the 1976 IWY report, "To Form a More Perfect Union," subtitled "Justice for American Women."

The 42-member planning commission appointed by President Carter to arrange these state meetings and a national meeting in Dallas included Former First Lady Betty Ford, editors of women's magazines, political and civil rights activists, religious leaders, businesswomen, and homemakers.

Only time will demonstrate the results, but as columnist Vera Glaser writes, "The women's movement of the seventies is the most recent phase in a groundswell to achieve the equality promised by the Declaration of Independence. It is reaching to the far corners of the earth, where other countries now hear the demands of women."

10

Same Is Never the Same

Set your hearts, then, on the more important gifts.

1 Cor. 12:31 TEV

The role of woman was fixed when she was created. [Members of the feminist movement are the] Pied Pipers of sin.

Spencer W. Kimball,
Mormon president

While we live in the earthly church under both the Law and the Gospel, it should be clear that the church is to be a living parable and a witness to the world of what the Kingdom of God is like. The church should pray unceasingly that it discover how to imitate Christ, not preferring one before another but preferring all and serving all.

Jan Larson, in 1973 presentation to LCMS
Commission on Theology and Church Relations

It is said that one cannot fall deeper than into the hands of God. I feel that we women have reached exactly this point. In the pain that followed the recognition of our situation, the Spirit of God touched us and we became bearers of God's vision of a new creation, of a new community in Christ, and of a new church that would be a true manifestation of the Kingdom of God. It is impossible not to recognize the Spirit of God in the women's movement, with its hope for a just and peaceful society, its recognition of the dignity of each human being regardless of race, sex, nationality or social status. We church women participating in the women's movement proclaim a vision of a new community in Christ that recognizes each human being as a child of God and therefore as a bearer of the image of God.

Rev. Eva Zabolai-Csekme,
Secretary for the women's desk,
Lutheran World Federation

You were called to be free. But do not let this freedom become an excuse for letting your physical desires control you. Instead, let love make you serve one another. For the whole Law is summed up in one commandment: "Love your neighbor as you love yourself."

Gal. 5:13-14 TEV

And so there is no division in the body, but all its different parts have the same concern for one another. If one part of the body suffers, all the other parts suffer with it; if one part is praised, all the other parts share its happiness. All of you are Christ's body, and each one is a part of it.

1 Cor. 12:25-27 TEV

WHEN THE ERA struggle is over, whether it wins or loses, the pendulum will swing back to more "normal" relationships between men and women. That thought is heard frequently in church circles today—and to some degree, there's truth in it, for the swing of the pendulum is certain, as history records.

One fact, however, must be remembered: Same is never the same! Even if ERA does not become law, women will not cease to struggle for freedom to be themselves. It's like the person who tries to climb the stairs to the top of a skyscraper. Even if she doesn't reach the top, her perspective is changed simply by the view from the 15th floor or the 50th floor, or whatever point she reaches. Her horizon is enlarged.

Not only does she have a new outlook, but mastery of one challenge, whether in whole or in part, leads her to try another. "Challenge is the mainspring of all human endeavor," says Lou Whittaker, a mountain climber. "If there is an ocean, we cross it; an ill, we cure it; a wrong, we right it; a record, we break it, a mountain, we climb it."[71] It's a part of our basic human nature, placed there by our Lord—or at least condoned and encouraged by Him—when He commanded us to subdue the earth.

It is improbable that the majority of women will ever again return to spending their entire lifetime as homemakers only. That does not mean that these women do not recognize the importance of homemaking and motherhood, just as it does not mean that the woman who has climbed the skyscraper will not want to continue enjoying the good things found at the ground level and meeting the needs which require her talents there.

The rights and welfare of children have important places in the IWY and UN women's platforms. Moreover, homemaking remains an option many women prefer, according to a 1975 survey conducted by Market Opinion Research at the request of the IWY Commission. In fact, only 5% want a career without homemaking as some part of it—but only 1 in 10 women under 35 years of age wants to be mainly a homemaker for life.

Half of American women think the ideal life would be to combine employment and homemaking, with time at home during the years their children are young, the survey revealed. Only 9% have never held a paid job, and only 6% never intend to.

"The major reason women leave their jobs is to have a baby," the survey reports.

> However, today's young mothers are more likely to return to work when their children are small than mothers did in the past. About half (48%) of mothers who are now employed and under 35 went back to work when their children were preschoolers, compared to 29% of employed mothers now over 35.

Perhaps one of the most surprising findings of the survey was that nearly two-thirds of all women agree that the government should assist in providing childcare on an ability-to-pay basis.

> Formal child-care facilities and services—day-care centers and nursery schools—are in relative low usage, in part because they are unavailable or have schedules unsuited to the needs of working mothers. Therefore, working mothers who can afford them turn to babysitters, while others work out schedules with husbands, mothers, and older sons and daughters.

Three other findings of the survey also indicate a move away from the traditional outlook. While a majority of women over 45 agree, the majority of those under 45 disagree with the following statements:

—It is better for everyone involved if the man is the achiever outside the home and the woman takes care of the family.

—It is more important for a wife to help her husband than to have a career of her own.

—If a wife earns more than her husband, the marriage is headed for trouble.

As the church looks to the future, therefore, it will have to prepare itself to minister, not just to women with a traditional outlook, but also to those with expanding viewpoints. As these younger and freer women grow older, their viewpoint will undoubtedly become the majority attitude. As they accept new and more responsible roles in vocational and educational fields, as they function successfully as bosses and leaders, as employers and employees, they will neither understand nor accept a church that says, "You may not serve because you are a woman."

And men will begin to agree as through experience they learn that working for a woman need not be frightening or demoralizing.

When a woman was named director of a department of 20 people in a church agency several years ago, the men in the unit became tense. Some were subjected to teasing, "What if she fires you!" Things went smoothly, however, and three months later one man confided to the female boss, "Just thought you'd like to know . . . I've stopped taking tranquilizers!"

When she intervened in a dispute that had been brushed aside by a male supervisor, a man who was involved called her after the matter was settled to say, "Thanks for helping. We've learned that when we talk to you, you listen."

Already many church bodies are listening to these "Awakened Women" and their male counterparts. A 1973 Religious News Service story reported, "The status and role of women in U.S. religion are on the rise. American women are being chosen for high national, in some cases international, administrative positions."

The news release went on to list Claire Randall's role as general secretary of the National Council of Churches; Jean Eckstein, president of the National Council of Catholic Laity; Dr. Marion Kelleran, chairperson of the Anglican Consultative Council, a global advisory body that includes the Episcopal Church; Rev. Florence Pohlman, a United Presbyterian, the first woman U.S. Navy chaplain; Sister Elinor Ford, superintendent of schools for the New York archdiocese, and Rev. Patricia Kepler, director of ministerial studies at Harvard Divinity School.

Women hold membership and office in the Midwest Association of Theological Schools, an administrative organization. In numerous denominations they may now serve as pastors. About 5% of all Protestant ministers are women, and Reformed Judaism has ordained a female rabbi. Although the Roman Catholic Church does not permit women to become priests, some parishes initiate them as "Extraordinary Ministers of the Holy Eucharist" or lay distributors of Communion. Roman Catholic women also may read the Scripture during the liturgy, lead congregational singing, serve as ushers and take up collections.

A task force of the National Council of Churches is reworking the Revised Standard Version to eliminate sexist language where there is no historical reason for it. The Lutheran Church in America has called for the elimination of "the ambiguities of generic terminology and the restriction of masculine orientation of language" in its theological and liturgical materials.

As the more conservative church bodies weigh their future approach to the role of women, their deliberations undoubtedly will center on two concerns: What does God's Word say on the subject? And, what is our responsibility in regard to God's desire that all should be saved, that disciples should be made of all nations? As Paul became all things to all people, "that I may save some of them by any means possible," so the church will have to ask itself, What is required today? What do the concepts of freedom under Christ, of oneness in the Spirit, of wholeness in the Lord demand in the religious realm of this world?

Freedom to the Christian means something different than freedom in the world. Christian freedom is not license to do whatever we wish, but freedom to serve. It is not absence of laws and restrictions, but voluntary service in gratitude for God's gift of salvation. It is love for others in response to His love for us.

Because Christ has liberated us from our sins, we are free to serve, free to use our talents to the fullest, free to be what God created us to be. Thus Christian freedom is more than liberation—it is fulfillment!

That, of course, is where the rub comes for some Christian women—when they feel called to a ministry and the church says no, what do they do?

A female layworker in a foreign mission field saw how hungry people in neighboring villages were for God's Word. In her spare time, she began visiting these communities, gathering the people around her and telling them Bible stories.

"She's preaching," said the male missionaries, and they sent her home. Fortunately, the bishop in America absolved her and sent her back to the field.

A Milwaukeean tells of the time her parish financial records became mixed up because of a real estate transaction. She worked in an office that routinely handles such matters. When she offered her assistance, she was turned down because women weren't expected to get involved in the business of the church. Eventually an expensive consultant had to be hired to straighten things out. "I could have prevented that—and I would have done it for nothing," she says sadly.

In the days before women were allowed to be Sunday school superintendents in some denominations, male superintendents who did little more than lead the opening devotions would usually have a woman assistant. She handled all the organizational detail. Before each voters' meeting, the man would then telephone the woman to find out what he should report.

Today there is still a hesitancy on the part of some pastors to allow women to lead women's Bible study groups. "They might teach something wrong," these pastors fear, forgetting the power of the Holy Spirit and Christ's promise that "where two or three are gathered in My name, there am I . . . ." Thus instead of the spiritual growth which could come from various women leading numerous cottage studies, Bible study for the ladies in such parishes is limited to a weekly or monthly session at a time convenient to the pastor.

Result: The women suffer. The parish suffers. The body of Christ suffers.

Perhaps the saddest aspect of this suffering is that it's all so unnecessary, for most churches today understand God's Word in a way which allows great freedom to women. In even the more conservative bodies, virtually the only restriction is related to the pastoral role.

The problem comes in practicing what our pronouncements permit. As Jan Larsen said in her 1973 presentation to the Missouri Synod Commission on Theology and Church Relations,

> When we stress civil righteousness of sex roles with all their requirements, we make ourselves a picture of the Law instead of witnessing to our freedom in Christ. When as a church we speak of women, it is what she is "permitted" to do and what her bounds are—a language of limitation instead of a language of possibility. What is then spoken is a special law *for women,* as though they needed some kind of extra guidance, as though the Gospel were not enough to redeem them. We hurt our witness when we define, openly or subtly, over half of our membership by their obedience instead of their freedom. And we are so blind to the Kingdom vision that we cannot imagine a woman as a representative of Christ and the church, even though CHRIST Himself sent women to prepare the way for Him.

At a 1977 Conference on "Women and Worship" in Madison, Wis., Eva Zabolai-Csekme put it another way,

> For a long time, women have been socialized to live in a state of numbness . . . where we heard the Word of God without really understand all its implications. We

> have been socialized to feel worthless, to doubt our potential and our dignity. . . .
>
> At a worship service it is impossible not to notice a significant discrepancy between the word that is preached and the word that is acted out in the structure of the congregation and in the structure of the worship service itself. The words in the Bible readings and usually those in the sermon proclaim Christ's message of liberation and salvation. They call us to a new community in Christ, where the barriers of the old creation are transcended and where Christ alone is Lord. They proclaim that in this new community the least become the most important and the powerful and mighty take last place. . . .
>
> Yet the Word that is acted out in the worship service says something completely different. In observing its actions we realize that the congregation consists of two classes of people—those with power and those without. . . .
>
> This is contrary to the message of Christ, which does not encourage us to dream of a new creation in the life to come, but calls for the transformation of our lives, our relationships, our communities and our societies here and now.

The consequence is that so many of the younger women of today see the church as a roadblock rather than a pathway. When Women for the Free Future burned a diploma in Berkeley (to symbolize their claim that the university failed to teach women anything relevant to their situation in society), they also incinerated a Barbie doll, a book by Norman Mailer (regarded as an arch male chauvinist by the movement), and a Bible.

The Bible speaks to all people, including these young

women, only they don't know it, and we Christians haven't made it obvious enough. The challenge before the church is to help these women hear God's Word, for:

—The Bible speaks of salvation, the ultimate freedom. Not only is salvation free, but we (women too!) are free to come directly before the Lord, without the benefit of anyone except Christ as intercessor.

—The Bible speaks of serving, the route by which we liberate and affirm one another. We liberate the lonely by listening, the sick with medicine and nursing, the unlearned by teaching, the hungry by providing food, the desolate by caring, the timid and hesitant by encouraging. Christ is the perfect model of service, and He says to us, "As the Father sent Me, so I send you." (John 20:21 TEV).

—The Bible speaks of justice and equality. It presents a God who is just, who commands His people to obey His instructions "without showing any prejudice or favor to anyone in anything you do" (1 Tim. 5:21 TEV). It tells us that before God, there is neither Jew nor Greek, neither male nor female, neither slave nor free.

—The Bible speaks of oneness and wholeness. There is one Lord, one faith, one God and Father of us all, who is over all and through all and in all. "When each separate part works as it should, the whole body grows and builds itself up through love" (Eph. 4:16 TEV). Wholeness is knowing who I am and what my talents are. Wholeness is being all that God intended me to be. Wholeness is being affirmed (something we all need) and supported in that role by all who are a part of the body of Christ. Wholeness is growing up "in every way to Christ, who is the Head" (Eph. 4:15 TEV). Wholeness is being empowered by the Holy Spirit, and using that power to build up the body of Christ." And so we shall all come together to that oneness in our faith and in our knowledge of the Son of God; we shall become mature people, reaching to the very height of Christ's full stature" (Eph. 4:13 TEV).

How can the church help women—and men—achieve this wholeness?

1) By affirming women as God's creation, and (like men) His fully redeemed servants . . . people placed here for a purpose (which varies according to their talents and abilities).

2) By carrying out this affirmation in word and deed, in the work and worship life of the Christian community.

3) By Christian nurture of marriage and parenthood, and vocational and voluntary service.

11

Everyone Is a Homemaker

Everyone is a homemaker because everyone, men and women, contribute in some way to the development of a home.

IWY Report

What Awakened Women want is respect and honesty so we do not have to roleplay or manipulate men.

The Lutheran

Obviously not all American housewives feel miserable and worthless, and it is important to understand why some women thrive in the role and others wilt and fade.

University of Connecticut sociology professor, commenting on a Boston survey which showed that women who work even as waitresses and department store clerks are happier and more satisifed with their lives then women who were full-time housewives

A woman should complement a man, not compete with him. It's a man's world and any woman who sacrifices her femininity in the game of competition is a fool.

Actress Arlene Dahl

Take "just" out of "a housewife."

Betty Ford

We don't want women to be the same as men, merely equal as human beings.

Congresswoman Margaret Heckler
of Massachusetts

A fuller concept of humanity recognizes that all men and women are potentially both strong and weak, active and passive, and that these and other human characteristics are not the province of one sex.

Jack Sawyer, Harvard psychologist

God created all human beings in His image. Some He created female, some male. Though each person bears some bodily traits of the other sex, each person is known as female or male. Through training and in living together we encounter the customs, roles, and rules of the communities in which we live, and we learn what is expected of female and male. Such qualities as gentleness, compassion, helpfulness, and artistic appreciation usually are characterized as feminine. Such qualities as assertiveness, vigor, initiative, and strength usually are regarded as masculine. Yet, they are human qualities found in both females and males, each found in varying degrees in each person. The deeper meaning of our God-given sexuality, which both separates us and attracts us, remains a profound mystery. We do not try to fathom this mystery. Rather, we accept and celebrate the mystery of our femaleness and maleness as one of God's gifts. . . .

The changing roles of women and men have particular impact on the family. God through creation indeed assigns the child-bearing role to the woman. The important tasks associated with child nurture, providing the physical and emotional necessities, and fostering the development of the child into a mature adult, however, require the efforts of men as well as of women. Family living should be an example of love, respect, commitment, sharing, caring, choices, and serving in accord with abilities, functions, and the freedom of each human being. Persons need to see that the demands of marriage and family living depend not on hierarchy, status, and power or weakness of male and female but on the maturity, mutuality, and wholeness of persons participating responsibly in the dynamics of interpersonal living.

Statement by American Lutheran Church
on Women and Men in Church and Society

The first lady has shown herself to be sensitive, intelligent, well-informed and poised—qualities that in no way detract from her role as wife and mother. Indeed, they enhance it.

Editorial urging that people heed the
example of the Carters "as we benefit from
their service as a husband/wife team"

A BRIGHT SMILE (the result of the right toothpaste), the correct hair coloring, and the new dry deodorant—put them all together and what do you have? The sure formula for a lifetime of love and happiness—according to today's commercials and advertisers.

Only it isn't that simple.

One-fourth of today's married women are not absolutely certain their marriages will last until death, according to Market Opinion Research. One-third of all the new marriages are currently ending in divorce. It's not just a phenomenon related to young marrieds, however, for nearly one-fourth of those women in the age 35-54 bracket who have ever been married have also been divorced.

Lasting marriage isn't a matter of love at first sight or "Light My Fire, Baby." Marriage is a matter of wholeness too . . . not wholeness of the individual (although that should surely be an outgrowth) but wholeness of the union and wholeness of the family.

It's a wholeness which is sanctified by God. "Marriage is to be honored by all, and husbands and wives must be faithful to each other," says the Lord (Heb. 13:4 TEV). He provides a pattern for the marriage relationship in His description of His "marriage" to His people: "Israel, I will make you My wife; I will be true and faithful; I will show you constant love and mercy and make you Mine forever. I will keep My promise and make you Mine, and you will acknowledge Me as Lord." (Hosea 2:19-20 TEV).

Considering the importance which the Lord places on marriage, plus its importance as a unit of society and its importance in the preservation of the human race in an orderly manner, it's amazing that marriage and parenthood are the facets of life for which most people have the least preparation. We go to school for 12 or 16 or more years to prepare for a vocation. We take classes in tennis, pottery, needlework, swimming, and a mile-long list of other avocations to prepare us for profitable use of our leisure time. We attend Sunday school, Vacation Bible School, released time classes and confirmation class to increase our faith and prepare us for church citizenship.

But preparation for marriage? Preparation for that lifelong (we hope!) relationship which so much influences our success in other realms? Nonsense, we say, leaving it to osmosis or instinct—or possibly a half-hour session with the pastor when the couple comes to set the wedding date.

We assume that someone who has grown up in a Christian home has observed the methods of Christian parents as they relate to one another and to their children—and therefore understands it all. Unfortunately children don't always observe, and parents don't always provide the perfect example, even if they are Christian. Moreover, lots of families in this country are not Christian, and many home situations are abnormal, with parents who are separated, divorced, widowed, or absent (due to jobs, recreational pursuits, or emotional abdication).

The church has an obligation to uphold the sanctity of marriage, not just through sermons on Mother's Day and Father's Day, but through classes—and not just for newlyweds but also for older-weds, for marriage involves change, and change can bring problems. A start has been made through institutes such as the Strengthening the Home workshops sponsored by the Lutheran Women's Missionary League and the marriage course developed by the Bethel Bible series.

When the LWML began its workshops, employed women took time off from their jobs, and full-time homemakers hired babysitters in order to attend—an indication of the desire for help. . . .

"Yes, help me cope with a marriage based on separation—for my husband travels two of every three weeks."

"Help me cope with the around-the-clock togetherness of a two-room apartment and two children."

"Help me cope with the isolation of suburbia where there's no bus transportation and we can't afford a second car."

"Help me cope with an endless round of coffee klatches and gossip, which result in neighborhood ostracism if I don't attend."

"Held me cope with a husband who strays."

"Help me cope with a full-time job and a husband who feels that any form of housework is beneath his dignity."

No, marriage isn't like it used to be in Bible times when God's people were a nomadic lot. Then boys learned at their father's knee how to follow in his footsteps as a shepherd or carpenter or tentmaker, and girls practiced homemaking and childcare from little on.

And marriage isn't like it used to be in pioneer times when the whole family braved hardships together as they went west in a covered wagon or homesteaded as a unit.

Nor is marriage like it used to be 50 years ago when families lived in close proximity to relatives, and women with small children could count on a helping hand and some adult conversation from a maiden aunt or a nearby grandmother.

What then does the church have to offer as a message to the married women of today? Several Bible basics:

1) A God who lives and loves us—and can be counted on to answer prayer. When we place ourselves in His

hands, He will guide us and never give us more than we can bear—that's His promise.

When we see marriage as a service to Him, our house becomes His habitation (a real incentive to cleaning) and our sink and stove become an altar where we offer our thanks for His blessings and our talents to provide for the family He has given us.

2) A mutuality in marriage based on dual submission, as we have seen earlier. In a Christian marriage, the wife is commanded by the Lord to love and honor her husband as head, while he gives his totality in love and labor for her, as Christ gave Himself for the church. There's an equality in the submission: "A wife is not the master of her own body, but her husband is; in the same way a husband is not the master of his own body, but his wife is" (1 Cor. 7:4 TEV).

We voluntarily agree to this submission when we take our marriage vows. We volunteer to limit our personal freedom in expectation of a higher good—mutual supportiveness and love—the acquiring of a helpmate who will uphold and encourage us, an enabler who will assist us to more fully use our talents and become all that God wants us to be.

The beauty of this unity, when practiced under the ordinances of God, far overshadows the responsibilities we acquire and the freedoms we lose. To have someone you can trust, someone with whom you can share your most intimate thoughts, someone you can count on to be there when you need him (or her)—that's the real meaning of helpmate.

It's a relationship of sharing and support, not of subservience. The Douay version of the Bible says in

Genesis that, in Eve, God gave Adam "a help like unto himself." The Hebrew word for *help* used here is the same word found in Psalm 33:20 where it says the Lord is our *help.* The picture is not one of a weakling supporting a powerhouse, but of assistance that is strong and capable and constant and comparable. It's a relationship of mutual dependence based on love, not oppression.

One woman tells of the time her husband was to give a speech and had forgotten his glasses. Without them, he could not read his notes. She had driven him to his meeting and returned home—a considerable distance. When he phoned to tell her about the glasses, she offered to drive in immediately with them. When she arrived, another man commented, "Wow, have you ever got her trained!" "I felt like slapping that man," the wife commented. "I brought the glasses because I loved my husband and wanted him to do his best, not because he demanded it of me."

3) A oneness, a wholeness that combines the differing natures of male and female. Sexuality is the gift of God, something to be cherished and enjoyed, as seen in the Song of Solomon. Sexuality finds its perfection in marriage, not in one night stands or the back seat of a car or an experimental orgy or prostitution. Its power and pleasure arise from shared tenderness and desire, not force or bribery or "proving your love." "A man should fulfill his duty as a husband, and a woman should fulfill her duty as a wife, and each should satisfy the other's needs" (1 Cor. 7:3 TEV). In marriage, the two become one—physically, mentally (working toward the same goals), and emotionally (cherishing and loving).

Such oneness demands maturity, and anyone who tries to achieve it through manipulation is doomed to frustration. Such oneness is attained through love that gives, not love that gives to get. Yet that is what some of the modern homemaker movements prescribe.

Explaining her "dos and donts" of "angelic" feminity, Mrs. Helen Andelin of Fascinating Womanhood says, "We pretty much have *control* when we are the kind of women we ought to be." Her advice includes: "Have a girlish trust in him; include some childlike things in your wardrobe; acquire a childlike manner; don't let him ignore you or insult you too far without expressing yourself with the charm of childlike sauciness." One would hope that when a man marries a woman, he gets a woman, not a child! And one would hope that when that marriage is blessed with children, the children get a mother, not a pal or sibling.

"Earn a place on a pedestal by building a noble character," adds Mrs. Andelin. Amen to the noble character—but watch out for the pedestal. A pedestal is a lonely place, mighty easy to fall off unless you let it cage you in!

A "Total Woman" leader tells the story of how her husband always dropped his clothes in a trail on the floor as he took them off. She nagged to no avail. Then she began admiring his body as he unpeeled. "It worked," she says. He changed? No, but they became happier. Since love means acceptance and not approval, she "accentuated the positive" and overlooked the negative—but she didn't eliminate it. Unfortunately a thorn normally continues to prick until it is removed. You can ignore it for a while but few have the power to be stoic forever.

In marriage, maturity is needed by both—the goal should be Total Personhood for both. If a man wants a mother to pick up after him, he's not ready for the authority of marriage. There are better ways for a male to prove his masculinity than by feeding it on the food of subservience. Women nag when men lack the maturity to admit their weaknesses, when men fail to lead with fairness and consideration, when men expect more of others than they expect of themselves. And conversely, men nag or become tyrants—or seek to escape—when wives fail to fulfill their responsibilities with maturity.

When two become one in marriage, the goal is completion, not competition; enabling, not outwitting; fulfillment, not manipulation; cooperation, not coercion; communication, not concealment; openness in conquering weakness, not evasion to overcome faults. In short, the goal is wholeness; the method is maturity.

4) An understanding of forgiveness. "There isn't a single sin nowhere on me!" That's how a mentally retarded Christian explained what Christ's death meant for him. Because Jesus died on the cross, the sins of all believers are forgiven in God's eyes. So often in marriages, there's a tendency to carry a grudge, to never forget a hurt, a mistake, a wrong that your mate did to you. But when we remember what Christ did for us, then we, too, freely forgive others. How essential this kind of forgiveness is to the continuing harmony of a marriage, since we are all human and therefore imperfect.

Fear of failure can immobilize us. Knowing that our partner will forgive our mistakes frees us to try again, to dare to be the "me" that God created me to be.

The Christian concept of forgiveness also includes repentance, a sorrow for what we do wrong and a desire to overcome, to change, to grow. It is in such growth—together—as Christians, that marriage finds its constant newness and challenge. A marriage never grows stale when two people are continuing to grow in Christ and in His service.

Children deserve such a home—where there is growth and love and forgiveness and wholeness. Children deserve parents who understand that they are the gift of God . . . and parents need to be reminded that children are the gift of God.

So often today motherhood is painted as pure drudgery. A young woman recently wrote to an advice columnist, "Why should I become a mother? I don't know if I could take it. What's good about it?" If they had it to do over again, most parents responding to a question in Ann Lander's column said they would not become parents.

So often parenthood does seem like nothing but drudgery. When my children were little, when the diapers were dirty, when one was sick and vomiting, when toys were scattered all over the house, there were days that I wanted to escape, particularly if the doorbell rang when everything was a mess! How great it would have been if someone at that point could have dropped in and reminded me, "You have the greatest gift . . . a life to mold, a life to nurture for His service. You job includes teaching, nursing, cooking, housekeeping, sewing . . . more skills than any one job outside the home. Yours tops them all! What this child will become depends largely on you."

How often I needed that kind of morale boost

during those few short years. Yes, now I know that they were short, but then at times they seemed unending. For just such moments, our Lord gives a great promise, "Train up a child in the way he should go, and when he is old, he will not depart from it."

Today my children are grown and a real blessing, particularly to me as a widow. If I had it to do over again, I would ask for the very same blessing.

But how can the church help parents raise their children to be blessings?

The obvious answer is by parent training courses, but that's only the beginning. Children need to feel welcome in the Lord's house. Children's sermons, children's choirs, parochial schools, and active youth groups are important.

So are nursery schools and day care centers. The ideal is for women to remain at home while their children are little, but with so many women today returning to work before their children are in school, the Lord has given Christians a glorious evangelism opportunity. Think of how many children from non-Christian homes can be exposed to God's Word through a parish day care center. ("Train them up . . .") Even for the mother who remains at home, nursery care for a morning or two a week can be a real blessing, particularly if her family lives too far away to babysit. (Even if they do live nearby, chances are grandma's employed and unavailable anyway.) Those mornings can give a young mother the time she needs to shop, clean the house, and regain her sanity through a few hours to herself.

If the church really believes in the preservation of the family, then each parish must ask itself, "How can we aid parents in bringing up their children? How can we help working mothers and fathers? How can we enhance the relationship between husband and wife?

Change is inevitable. The challenge to the church is to see change as opportunity . . . opportunity for evangelism and service, and for the future welfare of the church that evangelism and service must begin with the home.

12

That Women May Grow

I hope the role of women will continue to increase in the church. I am very proud to be the first president of The Lutheran Church—Missouri Synod under whom women have been appointed to boards, committees, and commissions of Synod. Every one of these women has served with real distinction and made valid contributions to the church.

Dr. J. A. O. Preus, speaking to the
1975 Board of Directors meeting of
the LWML

I saw my mother and many like her acting as the true backbone of the church. The church's behavior toward them has turned me away from anything other than worship within the church. How "put in my place" I felt at confirmation class when I found the church had no religious office for me. I know my place is not just in the kitchen—where then will the church find a place for me?

Response to questionnarie sent out
by LCMS Task Force on Women

Resolved, That the Lutheran Women's Missionary League encourage all women of the League to seek out and to accept the new responsibilities which they have been called to joyfully exercise within the organized church and in service to God and to His people; and be it further

Resolved, That we as women use our talents and energies to promote those organizational forms which encourage all of God's people—men, women and youth—to serve actively and to make the best use of the talents with which God has blessed them so that they can and will be a blessing to many; and be it further

Resolved, That we encourage our congregational, District and synodical leaders to nominate or appoint women and youth in large numbers to councils, committees, boards, or commissions at all levels of the organized church.

Adopted by international LWML in 1973

Whereas, The general view of the role and position of women in society is changing; and

Whereas, Women are becoming increasingly aware of new and significant roles that are open to them in the expanding life and activity of the church; and

Whereas, It is necessary that Christians appreciate the great gifts God has given to His church in consecrated and able women; therefore be it

Resolved, That all members of the Synod be encouraged to recognize the honorable position God has assigned to women in society; and be it further

Resolved, That the Synod ask those who are responsible for its publications to screen all materials so that proper perspectives on the role of women in society and the church are presented and so that stereotypes that demean or exaggerate the position of women are avoided.

Excerpts from LCMS resolution

"THE SPIRIT'S PRESENCE is shown in some way in each person for the good of all." So says Paul in 1 Cor. 12:7 (TEV). It also is a fact that no one has a right to mediocrity. Certainly mediocrity is no service to the Lord. Since God gives talents to women, it follows that the church has a responsibility to affirm women in the fullest and most appropriate use of those talents for the good of all. This holds true whether those talents lie in homemaking, motherhood, vocations outside the home, or service to the Lord.

What is the role of the church in helping women to live purposefully and joyfully in the home, the church and the world at the same time? In other words, how can the church fulfill its mission to the whole woman?

1. *Insist on accurate Bible translations.*

Affirmation depends primarily on words. Language is powerful. How we speak to people or about people can diminish or demolish them. Women have been diminished by Bible translations which use "men" for "people" or "mankind" for "humanity."

It is important that God's Word speak clearly to women, in the exact language of the original rather than with connotations unintended by God, connotations that have crept in over the years due to the cultural bias of some translators. Luther set an example of how it should be done. In his German translation, he correctly used the term "children of God" rather than "sons of God," which the King James and subsequent English versions have used. Churches today should follow his lead and insist on accurate Bible translations. Where the original is inclusive, the translations should not be exclusive.

2. *Churches should listen to women.* God promises always

to listen to us when we talk to Him. His church should do no less. Churches should listen to the needs, the hopes, the concerns of women.

"I believe that most responsible women do not wish to usurp the running of the church, but are interested in its welfare and therefore would like to share in its direction," commented one woman in a survey conducted in 1975 by the LCMS Task Force for Women's Work in the Church. In other responses, women said;

—*New attitudes are needed among some women.* "They must want to serve the Lord. Either they're 'too busy' or afraid to take any initiative." Several asked for seminars to "educate women in a role other than silence." Many women are very capable but just need the confidence to get started."

—*New attitudes are needed among some men.* "They seem to feel that anything a woman can do in church is no longer a fit, manly thing to do. Truly a crime! It limits the efficiency of a congregation and the mission in general."

—*New opportunities are needed for men.* "Men should share in Bible study and growth groups. The women are the spiritually alive group."

—*Greater interest is needed among men.* "As a child, I believed only women and pastors would go to heaven as I very seldom saw men in church." "There have been times when women have done the work and the husband has held the office in name only. This type of thing breeds resentment."

—*Widows and single women should have the opportunity to vote.* (The survey showed that in 38% of the LCMS congregations women were still not permitted to vote in 1975.) "Since my husband does not attend, I have no vote in congregational matters, but the men still expect you to support the church. Many times as few as 30 men make the decisions for a congregation of 1,500. Our money is good enough; so should our decisions be." "There should be women elders with responsibilities to/for single women, widows, and those whose husbands are inactive or unchurched."

"I'm highly educated, and I can *think,*" said one woman. Among the ladies' lists of wants were: the courtesy of airing their ideas for evaluation, opportunity to participate in the voters' assembly without the sense of trespass, and opportunity to have their opinions heard with respect and consideration.

Of the 3,090 who responded, 700 said they had no desire for any changes in their parish. Opportunities were rated *limited* by 466, *good* by 1,441, and *excellent* by 1,099. Twelve said there were *no* opportunities, and one said they were *unlimited.* Her comment: "Our pastor gives us complete freedom to express ourselves. Joiner or loner, feminist or conservative, nearly every woman can find a comfortable niche at our church."

3. *Educational materials are needed* which will incorporate the women's perspective and will help establish the full personhood of men and women. "We need Sunday school material that stresses the female heroes of the Bible and gives young girls ideals to look up to," said one response to the Task Force survey.

"Even though doors of opportunity may now be open to women, there exists a definite need for women to hear from the establishment, professional and lay, that they not only have a right but an obligation to use all of their talents for Christ," commented another woman. "Until sexist language and attitudes are eliminated from our services, educational material, and everyday conversations, women cannot totally experience the personal thrust of *the message."*

4. *The role of man and women should be given serious study* at pastoral conferences and theological forums, with women present as consultants. Women are requesting further study regarding the meaning of Baptism, authority, and ministry, and the implications of the priesthood of all believers as these matters relate to women and their responsibilities and privileges in the church.

In conjunction with this, there is a need for greater pastoral awareness of the total program which their church body offers to women. Many pastors are unfamiliar with the materials, program themes, and objectives of their denomination's women's organization. Some pastors attend women's meetings only long enough to advise the women how to spend their money and rarely stay for the program, particularly if it features a woman speaker.

Many still see a women's organization primarily as a group that cooks, sews, does handicraft, and a few service projects—and there's nothing wrong with an organization that limits itself to these goals, if that's what the women want. However, most women's organizations today provide outstanding spiritual growth materials and challenge their members to think about community and world needs which may be a barrier to the spread of the Gospel.

More women's organizations also are taking stands on national concerns, realizing that as Plato said, "The penalty good men [women too!] pay for indifference to public affairs is to be ruled by evil people." After a 1977 convention speaker reminded the international Lutheran Women's Missionary League of this statement, delegates for the first time in the organization's history passed two resolutions on public issues.

The one encouraged its members to write to broadcasting companies and program sponsors protesting open sex and violence on television and encouraged leaguers to commend broadcast companies and program sponsors for wholesome, worthwhile programming.

The other stated that

> We as Christian women should be involved in saving lives; therefore be it
>
> *Resolved,* That the LWML support the resolution adopted by the LCMS at Dallas "to support efforts by public officials and private citizens at every level—national, state, and local—to provide protection for all human life, including the living but unborn, under our judicial concept of well-ordered liberty," and be it further
>
> *Resolved,* That we encourage our members to use the educational materials on abortion and euthanasia available from the synodical office.

5. *Seminarians should have special training in ministry to women.* Women should serve as consultants in the planning and as participants in the presentation of such a course. Women constitute more than half of the membership in most church bodies. If future pastors are going to be able to speak to the needs of the majority in their parishes, they should be schooled in women's history, needs and concerns—and especially in what the whole Bible says about women.

6. *Women's bible study groups should be encouraged.* How

can we know God's will for our lives if we do not read His Word? Most women who join a church want to become more familiar with God's Word, but often they are afraid . . .

—Afraid to join a study group because the study commitment may appear to be for life. The answer for some parishes has been annual courses conducted in neighborhood groups which usually begin in January (when the doldrums set in for housebound women) and last only 8 to 12 weeks until spring (when gardening and yardwork begin).

—Afraid of revealing their ignorance about the Bible, particularly in front of the pastor, or afraid of being embarrassed if they mispronounce a name or word in Scripture. Once again the answer can be a cottage study group led by a woman, a group small enough to fit around a kitchen table. When I joined my present parish, I had been used to groups of 12—15 women. That way, if everyone contributed four or five comments, you could count on keeping things going for an hour or so. In this new parish, our young Christian Growth chairman said, "I'm afraid to speak in that large a group. We're going to begin neighborhood sessions with just four or five women."

Her idea worked! The women's enthusiasm drew other neighbors, and the groups provided outreach opportunities. In one area, a Roman Catholic woman joined and became so excited that she brought others from her parish, including a nun. The nun saw the possibilities and started similar groups in her parish. When new people join our church, they sometimes think our women are crazy. "You have fun at Bible study? Unbelievable!" Soon they believe—for when they try it, they like it.

Other formats can be successful too. In a Milwaukee suburb, 200 women attend a weekly Bible class conducted in a theater.

For employed women, the LWML has developed "Mustard Seed" studies, a plastic wallet of 30 single sheets, each containing a Bible verse, cross references, and some discussion starter comments and questions. These "Seeds" were in response to women who said, "So often at work we begin discussing religion and we never know what direction to lead the conversation. Help us!" Over 300,000 wallets have been sold—not just to employed women, but also as gifts for shut-ins, friends, and special occasions.

The value of Bible study, whatever its format and frequency, lies in giving women practice in speaking of spiritual matters. We often fail to share our faith because we don't know what to say. Instead we talk about the weather, children, inflation. Practice among friends leads to freedom in talking about God with those we know less well. Women's Bible study members often become evangelism callers—and LCMS education officials credit the LWML cottage courses with fostering an upsurge in Bible study thoughout the entire Synod.

7. *More theologically trained women are needed on the staffs of churches.* Churches which do not believe in ordination of women can meet this need through Deaconesses, female directors of Christian education, and trained layworkers.

When I was in a drugstore recently, a man approached the pharmacy counter and was visibly jolted to see a woman behind the counter. "Are you the only person on duty?" he asked with a red face. "Yes," answered the female pharmacist. "May I help you?" The man gulped, glanced at his prescription (apparently an order for medicine dealing with a male problem), and walked out!

I thought of all the times women have hesitated about talking to a male pharmacist or doctor about a female problem, but had no other choice. Regardless of how liberated women become, there will always be some, perhaps many, who feel shy about discussing personal and physical matters with a man. Like the woman who was going to have a hysterectomy—when she asked her pastor to call on her at the hospital, she described the surgery as an appendectomy.

Rather than laugh at such persons, we must remember that God has created each of us different—and respect such differences. Rather than try to force everyone into one mold, the church—and feminists too—have an obligation to consider all varieties of people. It's a wise congregation which encourages girls as well as boys to train for Christian service and which augments its professional staff with a female parish worker or director of Christian education. Many women will appreciate their counsel—and who knows, some men may also!

The hope of women—and the hope of the church—is that they may grow . . . in His Word, in wisdom, in understanding, in service, in love. As this occurs, women will experience responsible self-fulfillment that will bring joy and satisfaction to them and blessings to church and society. Not only women will benefit, but men too, for we are all part of one body.

13

How Do We Decide?

> As in all the churches of God's people, the women should keep quiet in the meetings. They are not allowed to speak; as the Jewish Law says, they must not be in charge. If they want to find out about something, they should ask their husbands at home. It is a disgraceful thing for a woman to speak in a church meeting.
>
> 1 Cor. 14:33-35 TEV

> Women should learn in silence and all humility. I do not allow them to teach or to have authority over men; they must keep quiet. For Adam was created first, and then Eve. And it was not Adam who was deceived; it was the woman who was deceived and broke God's law.
>
> 1 Tim. 2:11-14 TEV

DISAGREEMENTS HAVE ALWAYS been with us in the church. Disagreements are a part of being human—with our limited understanding we draw different conclusions, interpret from different backgrounds, establish different loyalties. It was that way in New Testament times when some said they followed Paul, others Apollos, others Peter, and others Christ.

Thus there have also been different understandings of the passages related to women in 1 Corinthians and 1 Timothy. Traditionally, most mainline Protestant church bodies in America have determined that in the administration of congregational matters, two principles must not be violated: "(a) women must not engage in preaching or in publicly teaching men in the church; (b) whatever participation of women in congregational affairs is granted, the principle must be upheld that women do not usurp authority over men."[72]

From the Pauline texts it is concluded that the order of redemption (which applies freely and equally to men and women) does not change the order of creation (and its application to the administration of the church and the relationship of marriage). Women therefore are to "keep silent," and avoid being disruptive or "lording it over" men. Man is not to surrender his headship to woman.

As these passages have been studied and restudied by church committees and conventions in recent years, insights have been gained which permit women to participate in congregational voters' meetings. These insights include such facts as:

a. It is impossible to ascertain from Scripture exactly how congregational affairs were administered in Bible times. The voters' meeting as used today in many denominations is an American creation.

b. Woman suffrage is not expressly forbidden in Scripture. Actually, nothing is said specifically about how selections or decisions were made—and voting is never mentioned. "Since no doctrinal point can be established except on the basis of a clear passage, the church cannot, on the basis of the texts discussed, adopt any binding regulations on these matters."[73]

c. The purpose of church organization is to provide the means for ministry and service—not the path to power. We vote to delegate authority, not to usurp it. No person's vote, whether man or woman, can control a decision. Women do not vote in a block, any more than men do. Parliamentary procedure prevents domination or concentration of power.

Consequently the only bone of contention relative to women, which officially remains today in the more conservative denominations, relates to women in the pastoral office. Such church bodies understand that statements of Scripture which direct women to keep silent in the church and which prohibit them to teach and to exercise authority over men mean that women ought not hold the pastoral office or any other office in the church whose function is to assist the pastor in the exercise and administration of the Office of the Keys (the forgiveness and retention of sins as outlined in John 20:22-23).[74]

With more and more denominations beginning to ordain women, the voices of those in the conservative church who support this are becoming more outspoken. Such persons point out that the New Testament services which Paul discusses were not the formal rituals of the Old Testament nor the liturgical worship of today. In the early Christian communities, there were no ordained pastors. The apostles provided guidance through letters and personal visits. Appointed elders were in charge, and the worship consisted of talks by those who were moved by the Holy Spirit. A prophetess could speak if properly attired.

> During such worship, questions arose with respect to the revelations given by the Spirit and proclaimed in the congregation. Paul insists that it is a disgrace for a woman to do this kind of talking, since it would be disruptive. He commands silence in this instance for the same reason that he orders the first man who receives a revelation to be quiet when a second person has such an experience and wants to talk.[75]

Thus those who support ordination of women say that these passages do not apply to today's circumstances any more than the requirement of a headcovering for women applies today.

How should such disagreements be handled? How shall the church decide? What should a woman do if she agrees with the doctrinal stance of her church body and wants to see it continued? And what if she believes it should be changed?

Three principles should guide us:

1. *God's Word must prevail. Scripture must not be violated.* Therefore, Bible study is essential. All who would speak to an issue must be thoroughly familiar with Scripture. They must consider *all* the passages which apply to the subject. Moreover, the passages must be used *in* context, not *out* of context. Where the meaning is unclear, other verses must be applied to bring clarity.

Sometimes the result of such study can be shocking. So often we read Scripture through the eyes of our parents or a favorite teacher or pastor. Often we totally ignore whole chapters or books of the Bible.

I remember well the response to an article I wrote on Psalm 150 and related verses. Some longtime Christians were appalled at the idea of praising God with trumpets and loud cymbals, with drums and dancing, with harps and flutes, with a *new* song! You'll turn the church into a sideshow, they retorted in shock and anger. "Surely the Bible doesn't say that?!"

2. *Those who serve in a leadership or teaching role must support the doctrinal position of the church body whenever they act in an official capacity.* Those who cannot do this should not accept such posts. People who join a denomination have a right to expect that sermons, instructional materials, and auxiliary actions will be in concert with the confessional stance of the church body.

This approach does not make change impossible but requires the following of prescribed and accepted processes for achieving change. All things are to be done "decently and in order"—God's people are to deal with one another in love and compassion, in fairness and trust.

3. *If you believe that the Bible supports a changed understanding in doctrine, work through appropriate channels.* Every denomination has these channels spelled out in its constitution or handbook. Usually such procedures involve submitting resolutions to a council or convention. This may lead to months or years of study and debate. Letters also may be written to editors, articles submitted to church publications, and outlines developed for parish and pastoral discussion.

If these methods sound lengthy, it's because they are! But trying to force an issue only results in dissension—and a poor witness for our Lord. As Christians, our goal must be peace and justice, not anger and dispute. As Christians, we must set an example for the world of how to resolve varying views calmly and patiently.

Patience. What a difficult virtue that is to acquire!

When my husband was elected to our town board a number of years ago, my first reaction was, "Wow! Now we'll get some things changed around here!" And in time some laws were changed—but over the years I also learned something: The changes which took the longest to achieve were the most lasting. In some instances, it took many discussions and many public hearings before agreement was reached—but the laws which were passed as a result are still in effect today.

Patience is also a must in solving women's issues in the church. By moving slowly, not only will the results be more long-lasting, but we can be sure our goals are God-pleasing and really of benefit to all women.

For instance, becoming carbon copies of male self-indulgence seems to be the goal of some feminists, notes Jean Garton in her talks to church women's groups. Liberation as women can occur only when we free ourselves from male criteria of beauty and success, she says. "Is to be like men liberation or degradation?" she asks, citing such facts as:

—Today three times as many women are involved in extramarital affairs as a generation ago.

—Lung cancer deaths among women have doubled in the last 10 years, due apparently to an increase in smoking.

—Drug use is increasing at a higher rate among women than among men.

—In the last 15 years, crime rose 380% among females under 18, compared with a 120% national average.

—The number of women who desert home and family now tops the number of men.

To follow in man's dilemma is like moving a lioness

from the zoo to the circus—all she gets is a fancier cage, adds Mrs. Garton.

Her point is well taken. Freedom to pursue popularity and position is a shallow goal, promising only short-lived happiness and often lifelong bondage. Being truly liberated depends on for what and by whom we are liberated. Being liberated by Christ for His service offers the ultimate freedom—for women as well as for men.

Yet freedom in Christ may pose a dilemma for the person who wonders, "Where does the Lord want me to serve? How will I recognize the door He wants me to walk through? What goal does God have in mind for me? How will I know?"

Decisions! Decisions! How do I decide? Even for the Christian woman, establishing priorities isn't easy.

However, just as certain principles govern the approach to change in the church, so there are ways to determine priorities in our lives and discover how the Lord wants us to grow in Christian service:

1. *Keep your eye on the ultimate goal—heaven.* Our pursuit of happiness in life and in service must not jeopardize our faith. When we focus on that final togetherness with our Lord, our joy becomes something to be treasured and something to be shared. We tell others about Christ. It's as natural as telling others about the $100 bill we found on the street. We become ambassadors for Him—and that can become a full-time occupation in itself.

2. *Pray for guidance.* After my husband died, I thought the Lord wanted me to continue in my part-time position as editor of a Christian newspaper. Then I was offered a job on the public relations staff of a large

treatment center for the retarded. I had never felt a call to serve the handicapped! After brief consideration, I turned down the offer.

A few months later I was again approached about the job—with more responsibility and a better salary this time. Was the Lord trying to tell me something? The newspaper I edited was in the midst of a circulation campaign; I felt a responsibility there—so my "no" was conditional. "If the job is still open in June after the campaign is over, I'll consider it seriously," I responded. "It may be gone by then," I was told. It was a chance I had to take—but I had not reckoned with the Lord's persuasiveness.

Weekends are always bad times for widows. One week in May, I had no special plans. I had been attending meetings almost every night that week and was tired. Simply to put my feet up and rest for the weekend would be enough, I thought. I was wrong. By 10 a.m. Saturday, I was lonely, bored, and overwhelmed with self-pity.

I found a prayer in a newsletter:

> Lord, send me a surprise.
> One that catches me off guard
>   and makes me wonder.
> Like Easter.
> Send me a resurrection
>   when everything looks dead and buried.
> . . . Send me a future
>   when it looks hopeless.[76]

Although I prayed that prayer over and over that weekend, there was no answer. No one called. No one came to see me. The depression continued. At last Monday arrived, but contrary to my expectations, the loneliness did not cease. The usually bustling newspaper office was almost empty due to illnesses and assignments.

"Oh, Lord, hear my prayer," I pleaded when the vacuum still engulfed me on Tuesday—my day to stay home and write. I accomplished little—and then at 11 a.m., the phone rang. It was that job again: "Marlys, we need you here."

"Why are you calling me today?" I asked in amazement.

"I don't know," said the speaker, admitting his own bewilderment, "except that my secretary, listening this morning to my complaints about being overworked, commented, 'I think today is the day to call Marlys.' " And it was.

3. *Analyze your talents.* Ask the Lord to give you the strength and courage to use them—or ask Him to give new ones. So often we have not because we ask not. Pray, "Use me, Lord"—but be sure you mean it, for the Lord will answer.

If anyone had told me as a child that someday I would be speaking to thousands at international and district church conventions and retreats, I would not have believed it. I was timid, bashful, and shy. I avoided college speech classes like the plague, and *suffered* through those I could not avoid. When I was elected a delegate to our district church women's convention, I did not have the courage to speak to a motion in which I was deeply interested. Praise the Lord—He doesn't give up. Today I know I can trust Him to provide the words.

4. *Look for needs.* They are there in abundance! In some instances a new role may require going back to school to develop skills. Colleges today are geared to welcom-

ing homemakers in the classroom, but the middle-aged mother whose children are grown should not overlook the professions for which her experience already qualifies her—jobs like being an aide in a nursing home, hospital, school, or Christian institution for the handicapped.

If a salary is not a necessity, don't ignore volunteer opportunities. Community programs and projects are crying for help. One person—or a few—can do a lot. For instance, eight women from Iowa visited Bethesda Lutheran Home in Watertown, Wis. Impressed with what they saw there, they went back home determined to help. They developed a cookbook, later compiling a second volume, and raised over $10,000 to pay for a new beauty parlor, barbershop, and clinic cupboards at the Home.

A retired couple in a rural church does "everything that nobody else wants to do"—putting up storm windows, cleaning cupboards, setting up tables. "We're so grateful," says the pastor and congregation. "We feel so needed," says the couple.

5. *Dare to risk. Open doors to the Lord's leading. Be willing to try something different.* Say yes if someone asks you to serve on a committee or run for election—in church or community. You may not win, but at least you'll be giving the Lord an opportunity to move you in a new direction if it is His will. Don't let fear of rejection deter you from applying for a job that interests you. Don't feel you can't do something new because of your age. Remember that Margaret Mitchell won the Pulitzer prize for "Gone with the Wind" at age 37. Margaret Chase Smith was elected to the Senate at age 49. Golda Meir became prime minister of Israel at 71, and

Grandma Moses began painting at 76.

6. *Believe in yourself,* not out of selfishness or self-centeredness, but because you are God's creation, because He redeemed you, because He placed you here for a purpose.

It's great to be liberated in His name! Enjoy!

14
What Now?

Insofar as the surge (of women to leadership in churches) accomplishes something like equalization of the roles of the two sexes in organized religion, one must applaud it.

If, however, it goes beyond that and leads, as it all too easily might, to female domination of the organized churches—if, for example, priestesses came to prevail overwhelmingly as priests and pastors have prevailed in the past—we think it would be bad for religion and for our society.

For one thing, it probably would lead to male abandonment of religious concerns and their responsibilities much in the way men have shirked many civic duties, secure in the knowledge that women will get necessary things done.

For another, it might lead to the enthronement in religious affairs of what Eric Fromm calls the "matriarchal principle (which) manifests itself in motherly overindulgence and in infantilization of the child, preventing its full maturity."

One recoils from the vision of a religious establishment—that is, the dominant portion of organized churches—advertently or inadvertently oriented toward the prevention of full maturity of its membership.

1971 editorial in *Minneapolis Star*

We are in a crucial period when the church in mission needs committed people eager to be in mission in every facet of their lives. And so dedicated women welcome every new opportunity for service that is offered to them. It was disheartening, when woman suffrage in our denomination was approved, to read and hear that "women will now take over the church." It seems that only in the church would persons willing to work and take on responsibility be criticized, while those willing to sit back and shirk responbibility are the offended ones! Let's make it clear, any time a woman takes over a man's responsibility in the church, there is a man willing to let her do it. When we warn women about *usurping* authority, should we not also warn men that God expects them to *maintain* authority?

Lu Greenwood

ONE DAY WE THOUGHT a retarded Bethesda resident had become lost. We couldn't locate him anywhere. A "missing person" announcement was put out over the intercom system.

Moments later he was found by a staff member. He was standing under one of the loudspeakers and telling it, "I'm here! I'm here!"

For so long that's how it's been with women in the church. For centuries, they have been standing on the sidelines, telling a deaf ear, "We're here! We want to help!"

Now at last the church has turned up its hearing aid—and that's good, for Christianity needs all the workers it can get. The challenge today is great. Three billion of the four billion people in this world do not know Christ.

Even in countries where Christianity has made great strides, there are still challenges. For example: Uganda. When boarding a bus to my hotel in Lausanne, Switzerland, during the Evangelism Congress, I spotted an empty seat next to a black churchman. As we began talking, he told me he was the archbishop of Uganda. In his country, he explained excitedly, there are 8 million people—and since 3 million are Anglican and 3 million Roman Catholic, that leaves only 2 million to be won for Christ!

Today Janani Luwum is dead. His killing at the hands of government leaders made international headlines. And what of his dream of a totally Christian Uganda? Will others carry on the mission?

In Asia, the challenge is to evangelize 98% of the people. Christianity has the least adherents on this continent, which is the cradle of the eight major religions of the world.

The challenge exists at home, too! Any church which has not grown 25% in the last decade has not kept up with today's biological growth rate.

Yes, there's work to be done—and women are needed.

Women are needed to tell the Good News right where they are. When Joyce Danforth, who served as India's prayer chairman for the Lausanne Congress, was converted as an adult, her heart was so full of gratitude that she immediately wanted to become a missionary. "Oh, Lord, why did you let me marry?" she bemoaned. "Now I can't go to a far-off country to share Your Word!" The Lord helped her understand that her mission was in her own community, and she has since been influential in bringing many to Christ.

Her faith is so strong that she came to the Switzerland meeting without money for a return ticket. "What will you do if the Lord does not provide the funds you need?" asked her husband. "I'll have to get a job in England (she had friends there) until I can earn enough," she responded. Fortunately Congress officials, when they heard her plight, had enough money left in the scholarship fund to pay for her ticket.

Women are needed to tell the Good News in foreign fields. The fact that Christians exist on every continent in no way makes overseas mission work unnecessary. Nor should the rebuffs we encounter in our own communities discourage us from sending workers abroad or going ourselves.

Notable ingatherings are occurring in Korea, Indonesia, Brazil, Chile, and a dozen other lands. Taiwan, which had only 33,000 Christians in 1946, numbered 650,000 in 1971. All of Africa south of the Sahara is in the process of becoming substantially Christian—in fact, Africa may soon be the most Christian continent in the world. In 1952 the area south of the Sahara had 20 million Christians; an increase of 30 million brought the total to 50 million by 1968. Never before in Christian history has there been such a gain.

Yes, the fields are white, but there is much sowing still to be done. In Europe, 90 million do not believe in Christ as Savior. In some areas of the Third World only a tiny minority is Christian—often only one in 100 or one in 1,000. In some countries, Christianity is limited to a few population groups (one or two tribes, castes, or economic levels). In Fiji, 90% of the church comes from the aboriginal tribes and less than 2% from the 200,000 East Indian immigrants. These "pockets" of Christians have difficulty evangelizing beyond their linguistic and ethnic boundaries. They need our help.

Women are needed to hear the cries of the world for food and justice. About 500 million people, 12% of the world's population, are malnourished. Couple this with the fact that 86% of the increase in world population is in the less developed countries, and the magnitude of the problem becomes apparent.

"Malnutrition is largely the result of poverty, and partly the result of lack of education," says the U.S. Department of Agriculture. "Poverty and illiteracy are worldwide, thus making malnutrition a worldwide problem. The key to better incomes, thus better nutrition, is to increase national productivity and to improve education."[77]

Responding to the pleas for peace and equality from the underpriviledged, Dr. Donald McGavran said in a presentation at the Evangelism Congress:

> The Christian church has good news for the awakening masses—that God the Father Almighty is just and intends to have a just world. The revolutionary impact of this simple statement should be grasped. It affirms that the very structure of the universe favors the common man. It proclaims that God intends an order of society in which each man can and will receive justice. This meets the deepest needs of the proletariat.
>
> Contrary to paternalistic thinking, the greatest need of the masses is neither aid nor kindness. Their greatest need is neither handouts nor social action; but a religion which gives them bedrock on which to stand as they battle for justice.

> The highly valuable gifts of the Christian religion are: God the Father Almighty who hates injustice, God the Son who died for each man of the masses, and the Bible which demands justice for the common man. The Christian religion endows every human being with infinite value. "Making people Christian," along with other things, means giving them a world view and a Bible, which irresistably, though often slowly, create equality of opportunity and undergird all strivings against entrenched privilege. With *this* wealth in hand, the masses can conquer secondary poverties. [One might add that the Bible offers the same hope to women seeking new opportunities to use their talents.]

Women are needed to help the retarded and handicapped. There are 6½ million mentally retarded in this country—a vast mission field. All too many churches fail to welcome anyone with a disability. Few have classes for them. Parents tell of changing parishes time after time until they find one where their retarded child will be accepted as a member of the congregational family. Some have left Christian churches because of ostracism. The developmentally disabled are "His Too!"

Women are needed as role models for young girls. Too many have parents who do not really care about them or are too busy with their own pursuits to spend sufficient time with them. The number of teenagers involved in drugs, prostitution, and pornography is appalling.

Women are needed to minister to middle-aged women who turn to soap operas and alcohol as tranquilizers when their children are grown and their husbands no longer find them attractive.

Women are needed to minister to men undergoing an identity crisis as they face the anger and competition of women. Women are needed to bring healing and reconciliation between the sexes.

"Ministries open to women are limited today only by our imagination and our own lack of concern for others," says Jean Garton. Her list of opportunities also includes the need for a ministry in language (to decrease the profanity which has become common in homes, TV, radio, newspaper, and all facets of daily living), a ministry to women with mastectomies, and a ministry to those facing terminal or frightening illnesses.

Yes the needs are there! Now how do we find the women to serve? How does the church get them involved? Most of us could do much more, and some liberationists spend more time demanding than doing. How does the right woman get matched with the right niche? Church growth can be impeded if we try to force believers into ministries for which they have no gifts.

Talent banks are one answer. People are asked to suggest women who would be capable and qualified to fill the increasing number of positions opening to women in the church. Those nominated are asked to fill out a questionnaire which is kept on file and reviewed whenever appointments are being considered.

Women's societies also are a resource for service, but the auxiliaries of the future may have to adopt new approaches, new formats. Leadership and planning most likely will be left primarily to a small core of homemakers and retired women whose schedules provide the time and flexibility for organizational duties. Several factors will have to be accepted:

1. Women who have worked all day in an office or factory take a dim view of long, drawn-out business meetings, where every detail of a forthcoming event is dissected ad infinitum. When a committee finalizes plans, they should be announced, not offered for discussion. Evaluations following the event can provide guidance for next year's committee.

2. Programs should be relevant, timely, varied, and interesting. Today's busy woman may opt for an evening with her family or some Bible study at home in preference to a dissertation on age-old religious platitudes, no matter how pious and true they are, and no matter how kindly and loving the presenter is.

"What are the needs of the women of our parish?" is a question every program committee should ask itself. If many of the members are office workers, a discussion on "How to get along with your boss" may be in order—or a topic on "Sharing Christ at Coffee Breaks." If several members enjoy art and needlework, how about a parish art show or a trip to a gallery noted for good religious art? Officers should consider themselves a success if they attract every women in the parish to only one program per year.

Some societies have adopted the circle plan, where all women parishioners are divided into circles according to interests or neighborhoods. The small groups meet more frequently and combined meetings become special events held only three or four times a year. The benefits include improved attendance and closer fellowship.

3. Women will attend only those meetings which truly interest them, but this should not be cause for dropping them from the membership roles or refusing

any privileges normally associated with membership. When one woman who had been an officer of her society gave birth to a handicapped child, the responsibility of his care made it impossible for her to participate actively for a number of months. She soon discovered she was no longer receiving her denomination's magazine for women. "You aren't entitled to it because you don't come to the meetings," she was told.

In some instances, the magazine and a thankoffering envelope or box may be the only link between a woman and the society—but this is still a valuable link. The magazine or newsletter gives information on activities, and the envelope provides opportunity for sharing her blessings with others.

4. Time of day and week will often determine who comes to the meetings. Elderly women may be afraid to go out in the evening, particularly in a city. Women employed outside the home cannot come during the day. A society may have to split into two groups—afternoon and evening—or else alternate meetings. Some areas have success with Saturday brunches (particularly if there are many single women in the group)—and Sunday rallies to which families are invited.

5. Every ministry is important, whether it be teaching Sunday school, singing in the choir, working in the kitchen, sewing for World Relief, working on society projects, or attending meetings. A woman who does one may not be able to find time for the others—but her interest in the church should not be subject to question for this reason. Some women, in fact, may not be able to do more than worship at church if they are

involved in sharing Christ through community involvement. In such cases the church for the time being has apparently fulfilled its role as equipper and enabler—but it should not renounce its role as encourager and expeditor.

To all of this, there can be only one conclusion. The Lord is calling each of us to serve NOW! This is not the time for women to be spiritual dropouts. They are on the brink of even greater opportunities. New channels of service are opening daily. If, however, the opportunity which you desire in the church is not open to you at present because you are a woman, that is no excuse for not doing the work that is available. It's all important because it is the Lord's work. It is He who placed us here. It is He who liberates us.

Grow in Him.

Be free!

Serve.

Rejoice!

Notes

1. Richard Wurmbrand, *Stronger Than Prison Walls* (New Jersey: Fleming Revell, 1969), pp. 33—34.
2. Ibid, p. 34.
3. Vern L. Bullough, *The Subordinate Sex* (Urbana: University of Illinois Press, 1973), p. 218.
4. Oscar Feucht, *Everyone a Minister* (St. Louis: Concordia, 1974), p. 34.
5. Ibid, pp. 34—35.
6. Ibid, p. 145.
7. Rosemary Ruether, *Religion and Sexism* (New York: Simon and Schuster, 1974), p. 141.
8. Herbert Lockyer, *The Women of the Bible* (Grand Rapids: Zondervan, 1967), p. 29.
9. Russell C. Prohl, *Woman in the Church* (Grand Rapids: Wm. B. Eerdmans, 1957), p. 70.
10. Ibid, p. 70.
11. Ibid, p. 70.
12. Report of the Commission on Theology and Church Relations (CTCR), *Woman Suffrage in the Church* (St. Louis: The Lutheran Church—Missouri Synod, 1969), p. 9.
13. Prohl, p. 60.
14. Ibid, p. 28.
15. Bullough, p. 34.
16. Humphrey D. Kitto, *The Greeks* (New York: Penguin Books, 1965), p. 221. (As quoted in *Daughters of the Promised Land*, by Page Smith [Boston: Little Brown, 1970], p. 10.)
17. Smith, p. 12.
18. Translated in G. G. Coulton, *From St. Francis to Dante: A Translation of All That Is of Primary Interest in the Chronicle of the Franciscan Salimbene* (1221—1288) (London: David Nutt, 1906), pp. 91-92. (As quoted in Bullough, p. 174.)
19. Bullough, p. 213.
20. Ibid, p. 218.
21. Ibid.

22. Lisa Sergio, *Prayers of Women* (New York: Harper and Row, 1965), p. 70.
23. Smith, p. 26.
24. Ibid, p. 27.
25. Susan Groag Bell, *Women From the Greeks to the French Revolution* (Belmont, Calif.: Wadsworth Publishing Co., Inc., 1973), p. 97.
26. Ibid.
27. Paul Lindemann, "The Woman in the Church," *Theological Quarterly* XXIV (Jan. 1920), p. 38. (As quoted in *Women on a Mission* by Ruth Fritz Meyer [St. Louis: Concordia, 1967], p. 15.)
28. Eileen Power, "The Position of Women," in *The Legacy of the Middle Ages*, ed. by C. G. Crump and E. F. Jacob (New York: Oxford University Press, 1962) p. 402.
29. Bell, p. 199.
30. Ibid.
31. William Gouge, *Of Domesticall Duties*, eight treatises, 3d edition (London, 1634), p. 275. (As quoted in Thomas/Aston—see footnote 32—p. 334.)
32. Keith Thomas, "Women and the Civil War Sects," in *Crisis in Europe, 1560—1660*, ed. by Trevor Aston (New York: Basic Books, Inc., 1965), p. 324.
33. Meyer, p. 17.
34. Lisa Sergio, *Prayers of Women* (New York: Harper and Row, 1965).
35. Edith Deen, *Great Women of the Christian Faith* (New York: Harper and Row, 1976).
36. Sergio, p. 3.
37. *New Catholic Encyclopedia* (New York: McGraw—Hill, 1967), XI, 143.
38. Deen, pp. 6, 7.
39. *New Catholic Encyclopedia*, p. 143. Perpetua's book was entitled *Passio Perpetuae et Felicitatis*.
40. Deen, p. 50.
41. Sergio, p. 22.
42. *Oxford Dictionary of the Christian Church*, ed. F. L. Cross and E. A. Livingstone (New York: Oxford University Press, 1974), p. 630.
43. Deen, pp. 11—12.
44. *New Catholic Encyclopedia*, Vol XI, 26.
45. Deen p. 43.
46. Ibid, p. 75.
47. Ibid, p. 82.
48. Eugene Baker, Henry Commager, and W. P. Webb, *The Building of Our Nation*, (Evanston: Row, Peterson, 1937), p. 57.
49. Deen, pp. 125—126.
50. *Collier's Encyclopedia* (New York: Macmillan, 1978), XX, 631.
51. Oxford Dictionary, pp. 540—541.
52. Deen, p. 164.
53. *Lutheran Cyclopedia*, ed. Erwin Lueker (St. Louis: Concordia, 1954), p. 10.
54. Collier's Encyclopedia, IV, 388.
55. Deen, p. 230.
56. Ibid, pp. 240—246.
57. Oxford, p. 1283.

58. Charles Ludwig, "Queen of the Reformation," *The Lutheran Journal* (Winter 1978), pp. 13—16.
59. George J. Gude, Jr., "Women Teachers in the Missouri Synod," *Concordia Historical Institute Quarterly* (Nov. 1971), p. 164.
60. Ibid, p. 165.
61. Ibid, p. 166.
62. Ibid, p. 167.
63. Debra A. Wilcox, "Women Initiate a New Era for Luther," *College Chips* newspaper (Luther College, Decorah, Ia.), Nov. 10, 1972, p. 3.
64. Meyer, p. 25.
65. Ibid, p. 47.
66. Ibid, p. 48.
67. Ibid, p. 50.
68. Ottilie Mueller, "When Mama Went to Merrill," Lutheran Woman's Quarterly (Summer 1970), pp. 26—28.
69. June Bundy Csida, "The Second Feminist Revolt," *The 1973 World Book Year Book* (Chicago: Field Enterprises), p. 152.
70. Ibid, p. 159.
71. "Freetime" section, *Waukesha Freeman* newspaper, April 9, 1977, p. 3.
72. CTCR Report, p. 6.
73. Ibid, p. 10.
74. This is also the view of The Lutheran Church—Missouri Synod. See CTCR Report, p. 3.
75. CTCR Report, p. 8.
76. Herbert Brokering, *Surprise Me, Jesus* (Minneapolis: Augsburg Publishing House, 1973).
77. "Is the World Facing Starvation?" (Booklet by U. S. Department of Agriculture, April 1975), question no. 2.

Bibliography

Bell, Susan Groag. *Women: From the Greeks to the French Revolution.* Belmont, Calif.: Wadsworth Publishing Co., Inc., 1973.

Bullough, Vern L. *The Subordinate Sex.* Urbana: University of Illinois Press, 1973.

Daley, Mary. *The Church and the Second Sex.* New York: Harper & Row, 1968.

Deen, Edith. *The Bible's Legacy for Womanhood.* Garden City, N.Y.: Doubleday, 1969.

Deen, Edith. *Great Women of the Christian Faith.* New York: Harper & Row, 1976.

Feucht, Oscar. *Everyone a Minister.* St. Louis: Concordia Publishing House, 1974.

Figes, Eva. *Patriarchal Attitudes.* New York: Stein and Day, 1970.

Gundry, Patricia. *Women Be Free!* Grand Rapids: Zondervan Publishing House, 1977.

Harkness, Georgia. *Women in Church and Society.* Nashville: Abingdon Press, 1972.

Heaps, Isabel Warrington. *Five Marys.* New York: Abingdon-Cokesbury Press, 1942.

Hunt, Gladys. *Ms. Means Myself.* Grand Rapids: Zondervan Publishing House, 1972.

Kress, Robert. *Whither Womankind?* St. Meinrad, Ind.: Abbey Press, 1975.

Is the World Facing Starvation? U.S. Department of Agriculture, 1975.

Landorf, Joyce. *To Lib or Not To Lib.* Wheaton: Victor Books, 1972.

Lockyer, Herbert. *The Women of the Bible.* Grand Rapids: Zondervan Publishing House 1967.

Mackay, W. Mackintosh. *Bible Types of Modern Women.* New York: George H. Doran, no date listed.

Meyer, Ruth Fritz. *Women on a Mission.* St. Louis: Concordia Publishing House, 1967.

Morton, H. V. *Women of the Bible.* New York: Dodd, Mead & Company, 1941.

Ockenga, Harold J. *Women Who Made Bible History.* Grand Rapids: Zondervan Publishing House, 1962.

Prohl, Russell C. *Woman in the Church.* Grand Rapids: Wm. B. Eerdmans, 1957.

Rossi, Alice S. *The Feminist Papers: From Adams to de Veauvoir.* New York: Columbia University Press, 1973.

Ruether, Rosemary Radford. *Religion and Sexism.* New York: Simon and Schuster, 1974.

Sergio, Lisa. *Prayers of Women.* New York: Harper and Row, 1965.

Smith, Page. *Daughters of the Promised Land.* Boston: Little, Brown & Co., 1970.

Tiemeyer, Raymond. *The Ordination of Women.* Minneapolis: Augsburg Publishing House, for the Lutheran Council in the United States of America, 1970.

". . . To Form a More Perfect Union . . ." Justice for American Women, Report of the National Commission on the Observance of International Women's Year, 1976.

Woman Suffrage in the Church. A Report of the Commission on Theology and Church Relations of The Lutheran Church—Missouri Synod, St. Louis, Mo., 1969.

Women and Men in Church and Society—Toward Wholeness in the Christian Community. A statement of the Sixth General Convention of The American Lutheran Church, Minneapolis, Minn., 1972.

Wold, Margaret. *The Shalom Woman.* Minneapolis: Augsburg Publishing House, 1975.

Zerbst, Fritz, and Albert G. Merkens, *The Office of Woman in the Church.* St. Louis: Concordia Publishing House, 1955.